BIRDING IN GLAMORGAN

Where and when to see birds in Glamorgan

Edited by

Alan Rosney and Richard G. Smith

Glamorgan Bird Club
2009

Published by the Glamorgan Bird Club - Registered Charity, No.: 1129684

First published: 2009

Printed in Wales by:
CopyPrint,
Treforest Industrial Estate,
Pontypridd CF37 5UR
Tel: 01443 844502
Fax 01443 844503
Email copyprint@dsl.pipex.com
www.copyprintwales.co.uk

ISBN: 978-0-9554483-5-5

Contents

Sites :-

Pomarine Skua – Bob Mitchell

Foreword by Iolo Williams

The first thing that struck me about the old county of Glamorgan was the incredible variety of different habitats contained within its boundaries. From the rocky shores of the Gower peninsula with its Chough and Dartford Warblers to the green parks of Cardiff, where three species of woodpecker live alongside Kingfishers and Cormorants, to the high moorland of the southern Beacons with their Skylarks, Ring Ouzel and Merlin, it is a birdwatchers' dream.

The problem for a mid-Walian like me was where to go to get the best birding. Should it be the reed beds of Kenfig, the Loughor Estuary or the mixed woodlands of the Neath valley? The answer, of course, is all of these and much, much more. Now, with the publication of this book, there is no excuse for not visiting the county and certainly no excuse for not knowing where to go.

The book is aimed at everyone who enjoys birds, from the casual visitor, the beginner, to the expert. It is a compilation of all of Glamorgan's premier bird watching sites, from well-known nature reserves to local 'patches', compiled by some of the county's best birders. There are sites here that I had never heard of, let alone visited, but they are places that I shall certainly be frequenting in the near future. This is a book that will inspire people from far and wide to visit this historic county, with the aim of influencing a new generation of bird recorders.

With its excellent maps, detailed information on how to reach each site and comprehensive bird lists, this is an invaluable bible for all birdwatchers - be they resident, summer or winter migrants - who intend to visit this unique county.

Introduction

Bird watching

Bird watching, bird spotting, birding, twitching, call it what you like, is one of the fastest growing pastimes in Britain. Interest has never been greater. The popularity of TV programmes such as the BBC's "Springwatch" is testimony to this. There are currently over a million members of the Royal Society for the Protection of Birds (RSPB) in the UK, making it the largest conservation body in Europe. The British Trust for Ornithology (BTO) estimate that there are currently 3 million participants in Britain. This is part of a national interest in nature and the countryside as a whole.

Concern has been expressed recently about the decline in the fortunes of many of our wild birds. Changes in farming practices, increasing development and the like, have put pressure on our countryside. At the same time as bird watching has increased in popularity, there has been a corresponding growth in outdoor pursuits such as off-roading, mountain biking and scrambling. If not properly supervised, such activities can damage habitats that are essential for our wild life. It is therefore vital that our network of National and Local Nature Reserves (NNR and LNR), Sites of Special Scientific Interest (SSSI), Wildlife Trust Reserves (The local trust is the Wildlife Trust of South and West Wales or WTSWW) are protected and conserved. The government now actually uses information on bird populations as one of its key quality of life indicators.

Why and how do people begin bird watching? Many start as children, their interest being nurtured by parents, teachers and the like. Others develop an interest later in life, whilst on country rambles and holidays. However you come to it, birding can be a fascinating hobby. But be warned, it can take over your life. To quote Simon Barnes, the RSPB correspondent and Times sports journalist, in his book 'How to be a bad birdwatcher.' *"I wasn't looking for birds; I am always looking at them. Not for reasons of science, or in the hopes of a fabulous rarity, or to make careful observations of seasonal behaviour - just because looking at birds is one of life's great pleasures. Looking at birds is a key: it opens doors and if you choose to go through them, you'll find you enjoy life*

2

more and understand life better." Similarly the comedian, Rory McGrath, in his book 'Bearded Tit,' expresses his passion for birds in a similar way, albeit in more vernacular language. *"I realised that birds have been with me all the time, singing in the background, hovering over key events of my past and sh****ng from time to time on the windscreen of my life."*

How much knowledge do you need to take up bird watching? The answer to this question is 'none.' It isn't always necessary to identify every bird that you see; however curiosity will probably lead you in this direction. There are many field guides available that help with the identification (birders call it ID) of the birds that you see. If you wish to learn more about birds, it is recommended that you join one of the local bird watching clubs or societies. These include the Glamorgan Bird Club (GBC) which covers the east of Glamorgan, Gower Ornithological Society (GOS), covering the west of the county or one of the local RSPB groups in Cardiff or Swansea. (Contact details can be found on page 190).

Having highlighted the importance of special conservation areas, it is a fact that birds can crop up anywhere, from 'hot-spots' such the Kenfig National Nature Reserve, to your own back garden. Even rare or unusual birds can occur in the most unlikely places e.g. Black Redstarts, scarce birds in Glamorgan, are usually found on derelict building sites and once bred in central Cardiff. Is it a contradiction to produce *a where to watch guide* when birds can crop up anywhere? Well not really, some birds are only found in specific habitats e.g. you will only encounter Red Grouse on heather moorland and Dippers are only found on fast flowing streams. This guide aims to help you find some of these special places, as well as suggesting 'new' sites to visit.

The modern trend of *twitching*, (sometimes called *listing* or *ticking*) has acquired a bad/comical reputation in some quarters. Most bird watchers like seeing scarce or rare birds and for some this becomes their main interest. Most birders (ardent twitchers included) do not spend all their time chasing after rarities and are content to watch the birds in their local area (maybe hoping to find 'their own' rarity). These bird watchers usually keep notebooks with sketches and notes on the birds that they encounter. These notebooks can hold valuable records of the natural world. Most birders submit records of their sightings to the County Bird Recorder. (Details on page 190). These records are then used to produce annual publications, such as 'The Eastern Glamorgan Bird Report' or 'Gower Birds,' which hold information on the current status of the bird populations in the county. These bird reports can be a useful addition to your birding library. Contact the Glamorgan Bird Club or the Gower Ornithological Society to obtain a copy.

About this book

In 1998 the Glamorgan Bird Club published a book entitled 'Where to Watch Birds in Eastern Glamorgan.' This included information on twenty-three of the 'best' bird watching sites in the eastern part of Glamorgan. It quickly sold out and plans were made for this, the second edition. Whilst some original material has been retained, both the number of sites and the geographical scope have been expanded.

Ringed Plover - Paul Parsons

Much of the information included in this book has been provided by local birders (See page 199 for a list of contributors), who have written accounts of the areas that they visit regularly and know intimately. The editors have made some minor alterations to the text but in general have adhered to the information provided by the authors. In most cases, sketch maps have been included, as well as O.S. map references. Where possible, details on access are provided, together with information on the nearest car parking, toilets, shops, pubs, wheelchair access etc. Each site guide includes some indication of the species that might be encountered, although these lists are by no means exhaustive. Some scarce species are mentioned, although details of rare breeders are omitted for obvious reasons. (See Table 2 on page 183). It is important to take the utmost care when observing birds, particularly during the breeding season. (See the bird watchers' code of conduct on page 189).

Whilst every care has been made to make the site accounts as accurate and up to date as possible, there will inevitably be inaccuracies and/or errors. The publishers cannot be held responsible for the information pertaining to rights of way etc. Please note that the sketch maps and are not drawn to scale. Any indication of distance is therefore only an approximation.

Why Glamorgan?

The old county of Glamorgan actually 'disappeared' in 1974, being replaced by the counties of Mid, South and West Glamorgan. Further re-organisation in 1996 resulted in the creation of eight Unitary Authorities, namely Bridgend, Caerphilly, Cardiff, Merthyr Tydfil, Neath-Port Talbot, Rhondda Cynon Taff, Swansea and the Vale of Glamorgan.

Traditionally natural history recording has been on a county basis. The Watsonian Vice-county system was originally formulated for recording botanical data and later adopted for bird recording in 1853. Books such as 'The Birds of Glamorgan' by Hurford & Lansdown and its predecessors used Watsonian v.c. 41 as their base. This publication follows their lead. It was felt that the Unitary Authorities were too small to warrant publications of their own, although the Glamorgan Bird Club is currently promoting the production of books such as 'The Birds of Cardiff' by David Gilmore and 'The Birds of the Caerphilly Basin' by Neville Davies. Each Unitary Authority has a section of its own in this book.

Dartford Warbler – Paul Parsons

An overview of Glamorgan

Situated in the south-east of Wales, Glamorgan is an irregularly shaped county that is approximately 75 kilometres from east to west and 40 kilometres from north to south, when measured at its extremities. It consists of three major geographical areas:

The Gower Peninsula

The Gower Peninsula is approximately 20 kilometres long by 8 kilometres wide. It protrudes into the Bristol Channel in a west to south-west direction. Gower is home to several species of birds that are scarce further east. It is an area of unspoiled, scenic beauty and as such was designated the U.K.'s first A.O.N.B. (Area of Outstanding Natural Beauty) in 1956. The peninsula is mainly low lying, although the central hill of Cefn Bryn rises some 200 metres above sea level. Gower has three distinct coastlines:

The North Gower coastline forms the southern part of the Loughor Estuary. To the west is Whiteford Point, east of which is an area of low lying salt-marsh and sand dunes that stretch some 10 kilometres to Loughor itself. The coast road provides many opportunities to study the bird life of this salt-marsh habitat. The walk out to Whiteford Point is one of the delights of birding in Glamorgan.

The south-westerly facing coast can itself be split into two distinct halves, each side of the rocky promontory of Worm's Head. To the north lies the glorious sandy Rhossili Bay, whilst to the south-east rise the sea cliffs that end at Port Eynon Point, a premier sea-watching site during autumn. Worm's Head or 'The Worm' is one of the few areas on the Glamorgan coastline to support breeding sea birds, although their numbers are dwindling. The cliffs also provide breeding sites for species such as Chough. An area worth exploring is the sheltered valley of Mewslade. This valley can hold good numbers of migrants on passage. Further east, Oxwich Bay has the only significant reed bed on Gower.

The south Gower coast stretches from Port Eynon Point to Swansea and has a series of scenic sandy bays punctuated by rocky headlands, the largest of which are respectively, Swansea Bay and Mumbles Head. These bays are sheltered from the prevailing south-westerly winds and as a result can harbour significant numbers of gulls, waders and other 'sea' birds, particularly after winter storms.

The Northern Valleys

The majority of the land area of Glamorgan lies to the north of the M4 Motorway. Much of this area lies above 300 metres and consists of a series of hills and valleys that run down towards the Bristol Channel. High above the valleys is the post glacial lake of Craig y Llyn, the highest point in Glamorgan at 600 metres.

The Glamorgan valleys can be split into two main groups: The western group of the Afan, Ogmore, Neath, Tawe and their tributaries, flow from north-east to south-west and the eastern group comprising the Rhymney, Taff, Ely and their tributaries, which all flow in a north-west to south-east direction. These valleys once held numerous mining communities that made the South Wales coalfield world famous. Whilst 'king coal' may be just a memory, the region is now being transformed into something of a tourist attraction with the industrial heritage at its heart. Many villages have the typical terraced miners' houses, often picturesquely painted in a variety of primary colours. This now forms the picture post card image of the valleys. These valleys are a far cry from the grim scenes of the 'coal age'. Since mining has gone, the rivers have become cleaner. Otters and Dippers have slowly re-colonised some of these streams and Salmon can once again be seen.

Areas of industrial devastation, such as the infamous 'Dante's Inferno' near Aberdare, have gone, to be replaced by areas of lush green vegetation and wetland that support a diverse selection of wildlife. The dramatic changes in the last 40 years are quite astonishing for those who can remember the past landscape. Restoration work has meant that the valleys are blooming once more. On the slopes of the valley sides and the adjacent hilltops the changes have been equally dramatic, due mainly to the commercial coniferous forests planted by the Forestry Commission. There are some very large tracts of forestry, notably Ogmore Vale and the St. Gwynno Forest. The occurrence of Crossbills, Siskins, Redpolls, Nightjars and even Goshawk owes much to the creation of these forests.

Many of the forests are not commercial in origin and consist of indigenous deciduous trees that are more typical of Welsh woodlands. Not all of the hills are planted, those that are not are generally covered in rough grazing land, rocky outcrops and bogs, these being virtually devoid of trees. The value of these rhos pastures, from a wildlife viewpoint, has probably been underestimated in the past. For example, a significant population of scarce Marsh Fritillary butterflies has recently been discovered using this particular habitat. This variety of habitat not only adds to the scenic aspect but also increases the biodiversity.

The Southern Lowlands

Just under half of the land area of Glamorgan can be described as low lying. Generally this area lies to the south of the M4 Motorway. A large portion of the eastern part is taken up with the City and County of Cardiff - the capital city of Wales. Cardiff itself has a flat foreshore, where mudflats attract waders and wildfowl in particular. The Taff/Ely Estuary was impounded in 1999 when a barrage was built across the mouth and the area was then renamed Cardiff Bay. From a wildlife viewpoint this was seen as a major setback, destroying an entire SSSI when impoundment was achieved. Some bird species have undoubtedly disappeared, others however have moved in, occupying the fresh water lake. To the east of the City, the Rhymney Estuary and surroundings continue to be highly important for birds.

To the west of Cardiff is the Vale of Glamorgan with its central town of Cowbridge. The Vale is largely made up of farm land with small village communities scattered throughout. This area is drained by the River Thaw and its tributaries. Much of the Vale, being private, has poor access for bird watching, so it is unsurprising that the majority of birding is undertaken along the 30-40 kilometres of accessible coastline. This area provides some fine birding locations, including sites such as Breaksea Point, Aberthaw, Lavernock Point and Cosmeston Lakes.

Further west, the area between Port Talbot and Porthcawl contains several nature reserves and includes the extensive sand dune systems of Margam and Kenfig Burrows, Kenfig National Nature Reserve and Sker. It was these low lying coastal sand dunes that attracted the steelmakers to this coastline and prompted the building of the Port Talbot works in 1948. Moving eastward, Merthyr Mawr dunes are amongst the highest in Europe and the Ogmore Estuary is an important, bird rich area, especially in winter. It marks the end of the beach and dunes systems. From Ogmore to Nash Point are the high limestone sea cliffs of the Heritage Coast that support breeding sea birds such as Herring Gulls and Fulmar. Here also is a colony of cliff nesting House Martins. These cliffs are the termination of several little overgrown valleys or 'cwms' that hold breeding passerines and migrants. The farms immediately inland are accessible and support a wide diversity of bird life.

Freshwater lakes are quite scarce in the county. Apart from the impounded lake in Cardiff Bay, three notable exceptions exist; Kenfig Pool, Eglwys Nunydd Reservoir and Cosmeston Lakes. Elsewhere, especially in country parks, there are a number of small lakes that are attractive for birds.

Off the coast is the island of Flat Holm, lying some 5 kilometres off Lavernock Point. It is a low-lying island, some 23 hectares in area, particularly known for its gull colony. Two other 'islands' exist, neither of which are true islands, as they can be accessed at low tide. Sully Island, to the west of Lavernock is a high tide roosting site and off the west coast of Gower is the Worm, which is described in one of the site guides.

Shoveler - Paul Parsons

Maps

The Ordnance Survey maps that cover the county are:

Landranger (1:50 000) 170 (The Vale of Glamorgan and Rhondda), 171 (Cardiff and Newport), 159 (Swansea and Gower) and 160 (Brecon Beacons).

Explorer (1:25 000) 151 (Cardiff & Bridgend), 164 (Gower), 165 (Swansea), 166 (Rhondda & Merthyr Tydfil) and OL 12 (Brecon Beacons).

Where possible, grid references have been used to pin-point the sites in this publication. An additional resource is the gazetteer on the Glamorgan Birds website (www.glamorganbirds.co.uk) Click on 'Birding Resources' and scroll down to 'Gazetteer.'

Key to sketch maps

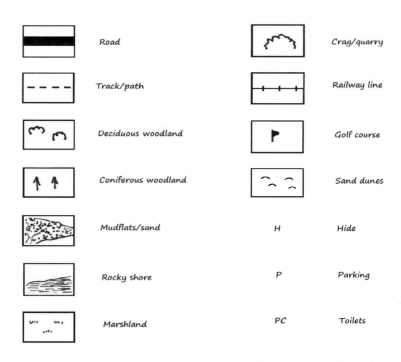

Road	Crag/quarry
Track/path	Railway line
Deciduous woodland	Golf course
Coniferous woodland	Sand dunes
Mudflats/sand	H — Hide
Rocky shore	P — Parking
Marshland	PC — Toilets

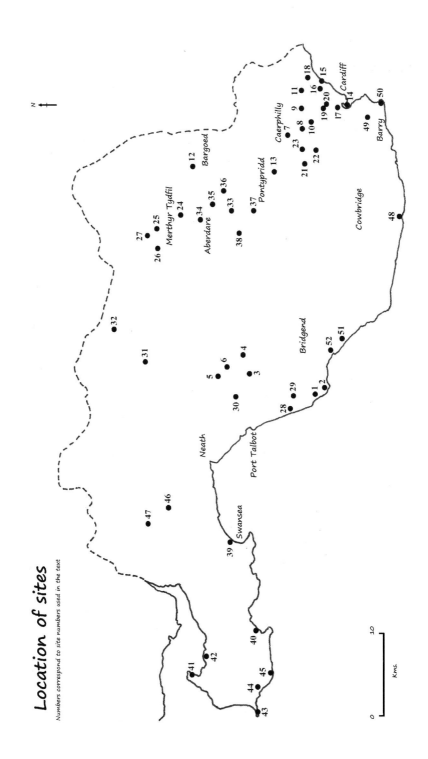

Location of sites

Numbers correspond to site numbers used in the text

Area1 : BRIDGEND*

Site 1 Kenfig and Sker Point
Site 2 Porthcawl
Site 3 Parc Slip
Site 4 Bryngarw Country Park
Site 5 North-west Maesteg
Site 6 East Maesteg

Lapwing and chick – Bob Mitchell

*Footnote : The site guides have been split into eight areas (The Unitary Authorities) which have been arranged in alphabetic order.

1 – KENFIG AND SKER POINT (SS 7981)

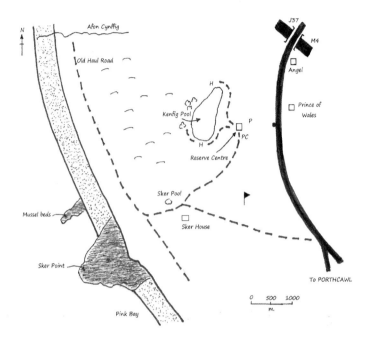

Access

For those using the M4, exit at Junction 37, Pyle. From here, there are a couple of alternatives, the easier route is via North Cornelly. Travel through the village and turn left at the crossroads. Kenfig Reserve is indicated by brown tourist signs. Cross over the M4, swinging right, past the Angel pub. Carry on down this road for about 1 kilometre, passing the Prince of Wales pub on the left. The reserve is on then on the right hand side. There are plenty of parking spaces provided outside the Reserve Centre and there are toilets in the building. A second car park can be found further down the road on the right. There are some hard surfaced paths but most of the reserve paths are rather uneven, sandy tracks. Wheelchair users cannot access the majority of the reserve. Generally the reserve is open-access, although visitors are asked to avoid the sallow area and reed beds during the breeding season. Two hides are provided, one on the south-western shore and another on the northern side of the pool. Wellingtons are recommended, as some of the dune slacks can

be very wet, especially in winter. Kenfig NNR can be contacted on
01656 743386

When to visit

Any time of year can be productive. Spring and autumn are
particularly good.

Kenfig is arguably the best bird watching site in the county.
There are a wide range of habitats that attract a variety of species,
ranging from wildfowl to waders and raptors to passerines. It has
been designated a National Nature Reserve because of the special
flora present on the site, notably the Fen Orchid. The pool covers
over 30 hectares and is surrounded by reed beds and sallows. It is
one of the few large freshwater habitats in Glamorgan. Between the
pool and the sea are the extensive dunes which lead down to the
rocky foreshore at Sker. There are numerous footpaths that criss-
cross the site, some of which cross the golf course. Check the
fairways as waders sometimes occur on passage.

The best time to visit Kenfig is early morning, as dog walkers
cause disturbance later on. Kenfig's position on the coast means that
it is a natural magnet for migrants. From mid to late March, migrants
begin to arrive. Wheatears can be found on the grassy areas near
Sker Farm. Later Chiffchaffs, Willow Warblers and Sand Martins
begin to arrive. By early April, Swallows and House Martins can be
seen flying over the reeds and pool. By the end of the month the bulk
of the summer migrants should have arrived. Reed and Sedge
Warblers are quite common. Late April is probably the best time to
observe the elusive Grasshopper Warbler. An early morning visit
may turn up a reeling bird behind the Reserve Centre. Alternatively,
check the brambles adjacent to the first hide.

In early spring Whitethroats appear to be everywhere, whilst
the more secretive Lesser Whitethroat may be found in bushes
around the pool. Whimbrel, on passage, may be seen in the fields by
Sker farm. Other waders can be found on the coastal stretch or
alternatively try the eastern shore of the pool. Terns are often
attracted to the pool. On passage, Common, Sandwich and Black are
regulars. Rarer Terns have included White-winged, Whiskered,
Caspian and Royal. Many of the ducks leave in spring although
Garganey may be present on passage. The site's reputation for

turning up rarities has been enhanced recently. Inspection of the rare birds table should whet the appetite. (See Table 2 on page 183). Perhaps the 'star' bird was the Little Whimbrel (Curlew) that was found way back in 1982. Since then there has been a succession of rarities discovered on the reserve. For example in the last five years alone, White-rumped Sandpiper, Temminck's Stint, Whiskered Tern, Black-winged Stilt, Cattle Egret, Laughing Gull, Barred Warbler, Short-toed Lark, Yellow-browed Warbler, Black Kite, Redhead and Brown Skua (See Appendix to Table 2) have all been seen.

A sea-watch from Sker Point any time between May and August can yield Manx Shearwaters, Fulmars, Gannets, and Common Scoter. A south-westerly wind with a rising tide is best, as it tends to push birds onshore. In September, look out for skuas and if the weather has been windy, don't discount the possibility of petrels occuring. The most remarkable occurrence in recent times was the "wreck" of Leach's Petrels in December 2006. Birds had been forced up the Bristol Channel by south-westerly gales and some 80 birds sought refuge on the quieter waters of the pool.

There are many breeding birds. Breeding warblers include all those listed above, apart from Chiffchaff. The Reserve symbol is the Stonechat, they can be numerous in the Gorse alongside the second car park and on the paths down to Sker. Linnets and Yellowhammers can be found, especially in the scrub behind the Reserve Centre, although the latter are becoming scarce. On the pool Great Crested Grebe numbers have increased in recent years and you may be lucky enough to see their spring-time weed dance.

A winter visit may be rewarded with views of divers, grebes and sawbills, all of which may visit the pool in cold snaps. For example, a Black-necked Grebe graced the area for a couple of days in October 2008. Both Whooper and Bewick's Swans have been recorded, although they are uncommon. From late autumn, look out for Bitterns. The best time to see this secretive species is probably at dawn or dusk. Most recent sightings have been from the southern hide (Arthur Morgan Hide). By scanning the reeds to the left of the hide you may be lucky enough to see a Bittern walk across one of the cuts. Duck numbers peak in winter with Shoveler, Goldeneye, Gadwall, Pochard and Tufted Duck being notable. Sometimes, many of the duck 'pop over' to the adjacent Eglwys Nunydd Reservoir.

Water Rails are often heard in the reeds but are notoriously difficult to see. Usually the best views are on cold winter days, when the birds have been forced to wander out from the reeds on to the ice. A tape lure survey in December 2006 revealed 14 rails in the reed bed.

On the dunes, Short-eared Owl, Merlin, Peregrine and occasionally Marsh and Hen Harriers can be found. Snipe and Jack Snipe may be found in the boggy areas around the pool, especially on the east shore. Little Owls are to be found around Sker Farm. The east shore fields can produce good numbers of pipits, larks and wagtails. On the fields at Sker, large flocks of Golden Plovers can be encountered, as well as huge flocks of Starlings. A juvenile Rose-coloured Starling was with this flock in the past. It may be worth scanning the finch flocks here as Lapland Buntings have been recorded on several occasions. A walk to the point might yield Grey Plover, Turnstone and Sanderling. Ringed Plover may be found on the shingle. At weekends fishermen tend to set up on the rocks and the waders are displaced. An exception is the Purple Sandpiper, which can be found on the mussel bed rocks. A rather underwatched site is the river mouth, mainly because of the difficulty in gaining access, nevertheless it can prove rewarding.

Recent ringing recoveries have highlighted the importance of the site as a re-fuelling spot for migrants. For example, the endangered Aquatic Warbler has been recorded on several occasions in autumn.

There is a Glamorgan Bird Club guided bird walk around the Reserve on the third Saturday in each month, being led by one of the wardens. Meet outside the Reserve Centre at 9 a.m.

Herring Gulls - Paul Parsons

2 - PORTHCAWL (SS 8176)

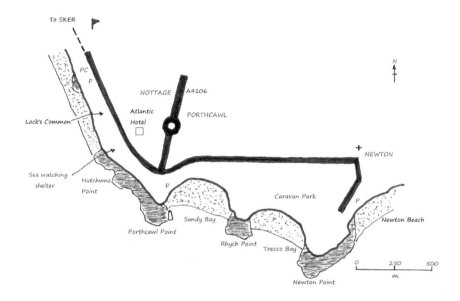

Access

The town of Porthcawl, with its sandy bays and rocky promontories can provide some excellent bird watching. It is primarily known as a sea-watching site. It lies on the northern side of the Ogmore estuary

If travelling along the M4, leave at junction 37. Follow the signposts for the town. There are numerous shops and facilities available. Car parking is relatively easy along the front. Wheelchair users should be able to gain access to most areas

When to visit

The best period to visit is in the autumn, especially following south-westerly gales.

There are three bays worth checking; Newton Beach, Trecco Bay and Sandy Bay. Being the quietest of the three Newton Beach is the most likely to turn up waders such as Sanderling, Dunlin, Ringed Plover and Oystercatcher. Similar species may be found in Trecco

17

The central area

The spectacular limestone cliffs of the Heritage Coast at Nash Point

Parc Slip Nature Reserve showing the regeneration of an open cast mining site

Contrasting habitats

*Bryngarw Country Park has
a variety of bird rich habitats*

*The flooded Alder carr habitat
at Forest Farm/Glamorgan Canal*

A view inland at the Ogmore Estuary with the castle in the background

and Sandy Bays although they tend to get regularly disturbed by dog walkers.

The south-westerly aspect of this stretch of coast means that Porthcawl is one of the best sea-watching sites in the eastern half of the county. When the winds are particularly strong, many birders head for the shelter opposite the Atlantic Hotel. South-west winds tend to drive birds up the channel and they can sometimes pass quite close to the shore. Gannets, Manx Shearwaters and Storm-Petrels are quite regular. In addition, skuas and terns can be seen in season. There is the outside chance of rarer species.

Lock's Common on the northern edge of the town can be a good place to find passerines. It is also a good spot to see gulls, as they often rest here. Mediterranean Gulls are regularly found amongst the Black-headed Gulls. The Heritage Coast Choughs have been seen in this area and rarities have occurred, notably a Richard's Pipit in 2000 and a Wryneck in 2008.

A 30-45 minute walk north from Lock's Common will take you to Sker Point (See the Kenfig site guide). The path is initially rather uneven (over pebbles) but then opens out on to a flat grassy area. This is a good spot to scan for coastal species. The path skirts the Royal Porthcawl Golf Course and overlooks both Rest Bay and Pink Bay. It was at the latter site that a Laughing Gull was found in November 2005.

Manx Shearwaters – Alan Rosney

3 – PARC SLIP (SS 8783)

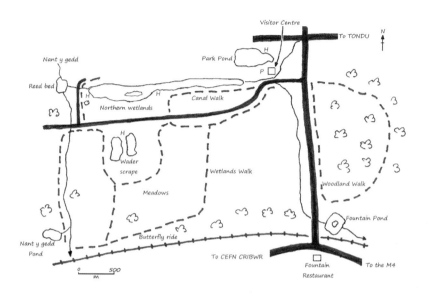

Access

This reserve is maintained by the WTSWW and is best accessed from Junction 36 of the M4 motorway. Take the B4281 and follow the brown tourist signs for Parc Slip. There is ample car parking outside the Visitor Centre. Tondu has a railway station and the number 63 bus from Bridgend stops at the southern end of the reserve, just outside the Fountain restaurant,

Parc Slip is a 125 hectare reclaimed mining site. It was managed in collaboration with British Coal from 1989, later being transferred to the Wildlife Trust in November 1999. It is composed of woodlands, wetland and meadows. Much of the reserve is accessible for wheelchair users.

When to visit

A visit is worthwhile at any time of year.

In recent years, 115 bird species have been seen on this reserve. In addition it has an impressive dragonfly list, with 20 species being recorded, including Emperor, Four-spot Chaser and

Scarce Blue Damselfly. Wild flowers are abundant and include seven orchid species, such as Bee, Common Spotted, Southern Marsh and Broad-leaved Helleborine. A series of walks (three are highlighted in the reserve leaflet) will provide access to different parts of the reserve.

Before setting off on one of the walks, it might be worth checking the bird feeders near the Visitor Centre. For Parc Pond hide, follow the small path to right of Centre. The Centre lies to the left of the main offices.

It is worthwhile picking up a leaflet from the Centre. All the walks described are shown on the Reserve map. The Canal Walk (1.1 kilometres) is an easy walk that follows the canal to the Northern Wetlands bird hide, returning to the Visitor Centre. Resident water birds seen from the hide should include Little Grebes, Mallard, Canada Geese, Mute Swans, and Tufted Duck, all of which breed on the reserve. In winter they are joined by Teal, Goosander, Pochard, Gadwall, and Snipe. This path attracts Green Woodpecker, Lesser Whitethroat, Whitethroat and Reed Bunting. Redwings, Fieldfares and Mistle Thrushes are often found in winter. At the Visitor Centre Pond, look for both Kingfisher and Water Rail. From the car park, go through a small gate to the right of the car park and follow the path alongside the canal to the bird hide. Leaving the hide, retrace your steps then turn right on to the track. Upon reaching the large rough road, go straight ahead onto a narrow tarmac path. Turn left then immediately right onto the wide track that leads back to the car park. In summer it might be worth checking for Wheatear plus Tree and Meadow Pipits along this path.

The second walk is the Wetlands Walk (4.4 kilometres). Begin as if on the Canal Walk. Upon reaching the large rough road, turn right, not left. Shortly turn left to the Wader Scrape hide. This scrape attracts Snipe and Jack Snipe in the winter. Further along the main path and on the right is a path that leads to the other hide on the Northern Wetland. Lesser Spotted Woodpecker has been seen in this area and the hide is good for watching Goosander at dusk, as they typically stay at this end of the lake. Alternatively, ignoring the path to the hide, there is a small gate to the Nant-y-Gedd stream that cascades down to the Nant-y-Gedd reed bed. Reed Warbler and Reed Bunting can be seen here and sometimes Cuckoo may be heard. To return, at the milepost, turn left along the cycle track, staying on this track as it bends left at the railway line. Cross the stile to your left after a short uphill section. Follow this track to a set of steps on the right. Descend and continue through the butterfly ride. When the bushes have berries, they attract good numbers of thrushes. Another set of steps leads back onto the cycle track. The monument on the left has 112 stones, one for each of the workers who lost their lives in the mining disaster of 1892. Turn left along the cycle track up to the T-junction, then turn right towards the car park. In summer there are likely to be orchids in flower on this walk.

The third walk is the Woodland Walk (1.8 kilometres). This is good for woodland birds including Buzzard, Siskin, Redpoll, Green and Great Spotted Woodpecker. On a sunny spring or summer day, this walk can be full of bird song. From the Visitor Centre carefully cross over Fountain Road. Follow the tarmac path for about 300 metres to a staggered crossroads. Pass the first turning on the right, taking the rough track (that can get muddy). The main woodland path bears right giving good views of Fountain Pond, where there may be Goosander and other water birds. The track ends just after the large memorial stone. There is a gate on to the main road. Turn right inside the boundary fence and follow a narrow path back to the entrance opposite the car park.

Mallard – Paul Parsons

Parc Slip is the headquarters of the local Wildlife Trust. Address - The Nature Centre, Fountain Road, Tondu, Bridgend CF32 0EH or call on 01656 724100.

4 - BRYNGARW COUNTRY PARK (SS 9085)

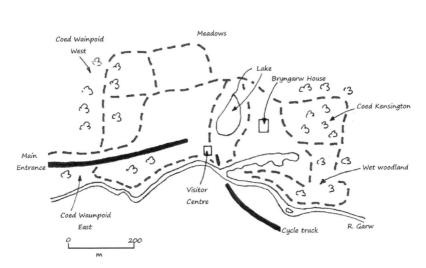

Access

Leave the M4 at Junction 36 and drive north, following the brown tourist signs. In Brynmenyn, turn right at the Fox & Hounds pub. This leads directly into the park. Information, facilities and site maps are available at the northern end of the car park. Most of the site is accessible for wheelchairs, especially the riverside walk and the cycle track.

The phone number of Bryngarw House is 01656 729009. The website address is www.bryngarw.house@bridgend.gov.uk.

When to visit

A pleasant walk at any time of year.

This is an extensive park, some 50 hectares in area that includes Bryngarw House, picnic sites and a play area. It was designated a Country Park in 1980 and opened to the public in 1986. There are several easy walks through open fields and woodland. The riverside walk and the cycle-way follow the eastern flank of the park northwards between the disused railway tracks and the River Garw.

Several paths lead from the car park into the southern woodlands past Bryngarw House. From there they lead down to the river and the cycle track. Another enjoyable route is to follow the garden's ponds on the western bank of the river. Take the paths through to the wetland or Coed Kensington and then back to the lake, meadows and picnic area. It is recommended that you scan the main lake and river as Kingfishers are regularly seen there. In winter there are numerous thrushes; Redwing, Fieldfare, Song, Mistle and Blackbirds plus dozens of Robins. There are also large numbers of Jackdaw, some Carrion Crows, Jays and Buzzards. All three native woodpecker species are present, although as elsewhere, the Lesser Spotted is difficult to see. The best place to search for this diminutive woodpecker is to take the path next to the turning circle and go up the hill. They have been seen (or more often heard) amongst the Beech trees. Green and Great Spotted Woodpeckers should be easier to find.

Lesser Spotted Woodpecker - Bob Mitchell

The woods contain various finches and tits. Goldcrest, Nuthatch and Treecreeper are present. Check for Siskin and Redpoll that can occur within mixed flocks. The river has Dipper, Grey Heron and Grey Wagtail. Although uncommon, both Goosander and Cormorant have been seen on the river in winter. In summer the woods are home to several warbler species. Wood Warblers were regular in the past but as elsewhere they appear to be in decline. Garden Warbler, Blackcap, Willow Warbler and Chiffchaff should be seen. Sparrowhawk and Buzzard are quite common and there is a chance that rarer raptors will occur.

Some common breeding species

Bullfinches are hedgerow specialists

*Goldfinches are now regular at nyjer
feeders in gardens*

Siskins are frequently found in the uplands

*Wheatears breed in the uplands but
may also be found on the coast*

Coastal waders

Winter brings Purple Sandpipers to rocky coasts

Redshank can be found on muddy coasts and estuaries

5 - NORTH-WEST MAESTEG

Hafod Farm Watch Point (SS 7889), Bryn Forest (SS 8191) and Garn Wen (SS 8492)

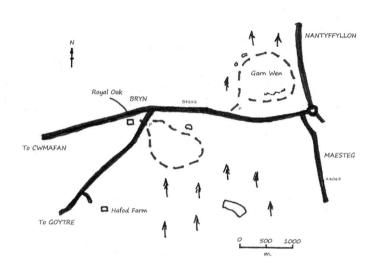

Access

From Maesteg take the A4063 north towards Nantyffyllon and turn left along the B4282 towards Bryn or from Port Talbot, take the A4107 north and follow the B4282 from Cwmafan. An alternative, accessing Hafod Farm, is to take the right turn in Port Talbot at Taibach Rugby Club. The narrow road then passes underneath the motorway. After passing through the village of Goytre, continue along the lane for approximately 2 kilometres. Hafod Farm is on the right, where a farm track leads up through the forestry to a watch-point overlooking the farm.
[Do not enter the farm, as it is private land].

From Hafod Farm continue north-west on the Bryn Road for about 3-4 kilometres. In Bryn, turn immediately right at the Royal Oak public house. Continue for a short distance up the hill. At the junction, cross over in to Station Terrace. Ignore the no-through road signs and at the end of the lane there is a small car park. Wheelchair users could access some of the areas mentioned.

Garn Wen lies a further 2 kilometres east along the B4282. Parking is available opposite the golf course. A network of forestry tracks runs around the mountain to the top.

When to visit
Any time of year, although spring is probably best.

These upland sites can provide some excellent birding. Coniferous forests tend to dominate. Hafod Farm is a convenient watch-point. Scan the tree tops in spring for a chance of seeing displaying Goshawk. From the elevated position other canopy dwellers such as Crossbill, Siskin and Redpoll are possible and with luck, Lesser Spotted Woodpecker might be seen.

There is a large area of coniferous forestry to the south of Bryn with Larch dominant. There are several walks where typical woodland species should be encountered e.g. Buzzard, Goshawk, Siskin, Crossbill, Jay, Nuthatch and woodpeckers. There are breeding Willow Warblers, Chiffchaff, Tree Pipit, Sparrowhawk, Whinchat, Redpoll, Cuckoo and Whitethroat in the area. There has been some clear-felling which may prove attractive for species such as Nightjar and Tree Pipit. Great Grey Shrikes have over-wintered in clearings in the past.

Garn Wen mountain holds similar species. In addition to the species listed above, there are Woodcock and Grasshopper Warbler. The raptor list for this site is quite impressive with Long-eared Owl, Merlin, Buzzard, Peregrine and Sparrowhawk all being recorded.

Barn Owl – Bob Mitchell

6 - EAST MAESTEG
Darren Woods (SS 8789) and Mynydd Bach (SS 8692)

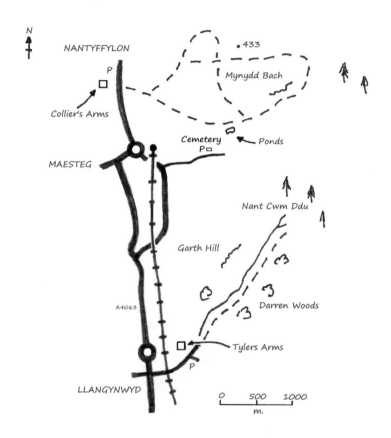

Access

     Darren Woods lie close to the village of Llangynwyd on the A4063 Maesteg road. A minor road runs east from the crossroads in Llangynwyd Square to Pont Rhyd-y-Cyff. There is a car park opposite the Tylers Arms. A footpath leads into the woods. Mynydd Bach lies further north in Nantyfyllon. There are two access points. Park in the Cemetery; follow the minor road along the new road leading to Cwrt y Mwnws Farm. There are several paths leading off this road on to the hill. Alternatively park in Nantyffyllon, from the Collier's Arms, cross the footbridge and railway line. Go up the steps to the disused railway line and bear left for 1 kilometre. Follow the concrete road up to the dragonfly ponds. There are further footpaths on to the mountain. Wheelchair use would be impossible.

When to visit
Probably best in spring and summer.

Darren Woods have a good variety of woodland species, including many of the Welsh upland specialities. The area has a mixture of deciduous and coniferous woodland with open hillsides beyond. The site list is impressive with Redstart, Pied Flycatcher, Spotted Flycatcher, Wood Warbler, Garden Warbler, Marsh Tit and all three woodpeckers being recorded. On the hillsides Tree Pipit and Cuckoo are possible and Whinchat is still holding on in this area. In the conifers look for Crossbill, Siskin and Redpoll.

Mynydd Bach is typical open moorland habitat. It has a mixture of farmland, moorland and crags. Breeding Meadow Pipit, Skylark, Wheatear, Yellowhammer, Reed Bunting and Stonechat can be found. Recently Dartford Warblers have been seen in the area. The crags hold Raven and Buzzard. There have been occasional sightings of Woodcock, Goshawk, Little Owl, Peregrine, Merlin and Golden Plover.

Whilst in the area it might be worthwhile checking Maesteg Cemetery. In winter, thrushes are often encountered here and rarities such as Ring Ouzel, Firecrest and Yellow-browed Warbler have been encountered on passage.

Area 2 : CAERPHILLY

Site 7 Caerphilly Castle Moat
Site 8 Caerphilly Mountain
Site 9 Rudry
Site 10 Parc Cefn Onn
Site 11 Caerphilly Ridgeway
Site 12 Parc Cwm Darran
Site 13 Nelson

Great Crested Grebe and chicks – Bob Mitchell

7 - CAERPHILLY CASTLE MOAT (ST 1587)

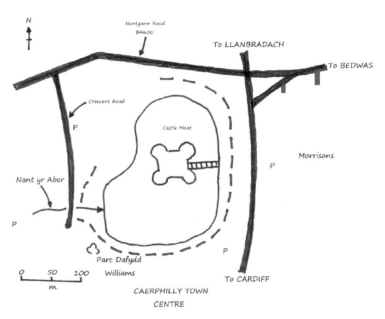

Access

Caerphilly lies some 8 kilometres north of Cardiff. Take the A470 Merthyr road north and turn off for Caerphilly at the Nantgarw exit (A468). Go past the GE works to the roundabout at Penrhos. Ignoring the Caerphilly by-pass, take the B4600 past the Cwrt Rawlin pub. Go straight on at the St. Martins Farm traffic lights and the Castle is about 1 kilometre further up the road on the right. There is a one-way traffic system. The Castle is situated in the middle of Caerphilly and is easily accessible. Wheelchair access is possible in most areas, as the paths are well maintained. There are three car parks available. The car parks at the Twyn and to the rear of Crescent Road are pay and display, whilst the Morrisons car park is free, although there is a time limit and wardens patrol the site. There are a few roadside parking places in Crescent Road, although there are rarely spaces available. The bus and train stations are situated at the 'top' (south) of the town, some 200-300 metres away - walk down the main street and the castle is on your left. There are numerous facilities in the town.

When to visit

Winter is the best time to visit this area.

The moat provides an extensive area of fresh, shallow water that attracts good numbers of ducks, geese and gulls. The birds are used to people and often afford very good views and photo opportunities. There are some islands and scrub areas that are worth checking. The landscaped grounds that surround the Castle, especially Parc Dafydd Williams, on the southern side of the Castle can be interesting. Probably the best area of water to scan is to the rear of the Castle, where there is an open vista.

Apart from the ever present Mallard, other duck species may be seen. Tufted Duck appear in winter, though numbers have fallen recently, possibly as a result of the silting up of the Moat. Other species that may be encountered are Pochard, Teal and Wigeon. Little Grebe have been recorded in past winters, as have Great Crested Grebes. They tend to favour the Nantgarw Road (northern) side of the Moat. An unusual visitor was a drake Mandarin Duck that appeared in October 2005.

It is worth checking out the gulls. The majority are Black-headed but Common, Lesser and Great Black-backs can also be seen. The site has sometimes attracted scarce visitors such as Mediterranean Gull. As on most water bodies, Coot and Moorhen are ever present. On the islands, Water Rail are found but are very difficult to see. Pied Wagtails are usually found on the paths and grassy banks. Sometimes Grey Wagtails and Kingfisher may also be seen. Check the Nant yr Aber stream that enters the moat on its western side. Surprisingly a Little Egret visited the site in May 2004. Scan the Castle walls: Peregrine, Sparrowhawk and Grey Heron have been seen perching there in the past. Pigeons and Jackdaws also use the castle walls for nesting. Migrants such as Swallows and House Martins are particularly attracted to the site. Surprisingly, Common and Black Terns and Kittiwake have all visited.

The moat is not particularly productive in summer as there is a lot of disturbance. You cannot miss the resident Greylag and Canada Geese. Recently a Sand Martin colony has been established. The martins can often be seen skimming over the northern section of the moat.

8 - CAERPHILLY MOUNTAIN
Caerphilly Common (ST 1585) and The Warren (ST 1685)

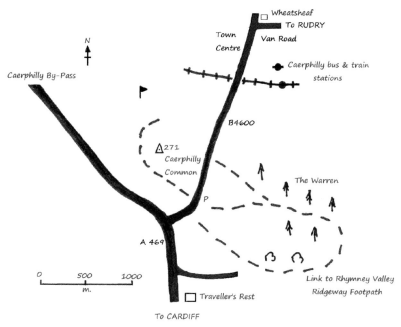

Access

There are numerous bird watching opportunities along the Caerphilly Ridgeway. Running approximately east – west, this ridge forms the southern rim of the South Wales coalfield and acts as a dividing line between the valleys to the north and the coastal plain to the south. The Common is a well known spot overlooking the town of Caerphilly to the north. Much of this area can be accessed via the Rhymney Valley Ridgeway Path.

To reach Caerphilly Common and the Warren from Caerphilly, take the mountain road, past the Caerphilly Golf Club, south of the town. The road rises steeply, until it reaches the summit at 271metres above sea level.

From Cardiff, take the A469 towards Caerphilly, past the Traveller's Rest pub on your right. There is a car park at the top of the mountain, next to a snack bar. Unfortunately few of the footpaths are accessible for wheelchairs. There are no toilets in the area.

When to visit

Summer is probably the best season, although autumn and winter can be interesting.

There are numerous walks, two are described.below :

The first crosses the road from the snack bar car park and leads on to the mountain. Bracken appears to be taking over this area and the floral interest of the site has consequently diminshed. On fine summer days this path can get very busy, making birding rather difficult. An early morning start is therefore recommended. Perseverance can bring Meadow Pipit, Linnet, Skylark, Stonechat and in summer, Whitethroat. In the past Grasshopper Warblers have occurred in the boggy areas to the south of the site. In May 2002, a Nightingale, a very rare bird in the region, was singing in the garden of an abandoned cottage building. Buzzards are ever present and Kestrel is also possible. Cuckoos were formerly common here but as elsewhere they are becoming scarce. Continue on the path to a fine viewpoint, overlooking Caerphilly Golf Course and the town. This is a good spot to scan for raptors. Hobby has been recorded in summer.

The second path leads from the rear of the snack bar to 'The Warren.' Bracken is also encroaching on to this site. The path drops steeply down into a small valley. It can prove rather difficult, particularly after heavy rain and wellingtons are recommended. This area is lightly wooded with a mixture of conifers and deciduous trees. These can yield typical woodland species such as Redstart, Siskin, Goldcrest and various tits. The yaffle of the Green Woodpecker is commonly heard here. In winter, Woodcock are sometimes flushed from boggy ground on the woodland edges. In the past, the clearings held Nightjar in the summer but unfortunately they have not been seen or heard for some years. The farm at the base of the valley has a reedy pond which attracts Mallard, Grey Heron and Moorhen. In the wooded areas Tawny Owls, Carrion Crows and Raven are found and Crossbills are also possible in the conifers. Buzzards seem to be doing well here and there is usually a pair present. From here you have the choice of returning to the car park or taking the option of continuing along the Ridgeway Path towards Rudry. The latter has several overgrown quarries and clay pits where Adders are often seen basking in sunny spots.

9 – RUDRY
Wern Ddu (ST 1785) and Rudry Common (ST 1886)

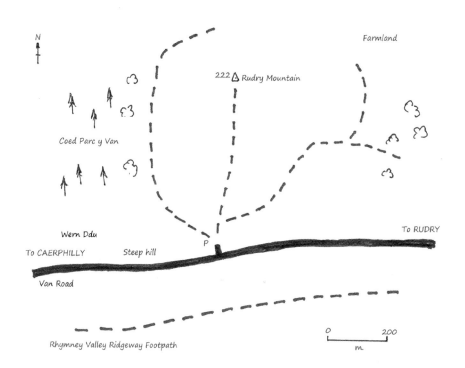

Access

From Caerphilly town centre, turn into Van Road, alongside the Wheatsheaf pub. Continue on this road for about 1 kilometre, past the Harold Wilson Industrial Estate on the right. Travelling up the hill, pass through the coniferous woods that lead into more open moorland habitat. Before this, notice the old lime kilns on the right hand side. The best way to explore the area is to park in the Rudry Common car park, which is on the left at ST 182865. There is a site map in this car park. Beware car thieves have been operating in the area. There are several well marked footpaths which can be quite uneven at times. The site has a lot to interest archaeologists with several old bell pits dotted about. These are rather overgrown and are quite deep. The nearest toilets are in Caerphilly or in the Maenllwyd pub in Rudry. Wheelchair users will not be able to access the paths. The future of the site is rather uncertain as it has been up for sale recently.

When to visit

Spring is probably best. Early morning is recommended as off-road bikers can cause disturbance later on in the day

On Rudry Mountain, there are two distinct habitats to explore. By branching off right from the car park there is open heath land with isolated Birch, Gorse and Willow. As at Caerphilly Common, Bracken appears to be taking over the site. Spring or early summer is the best time to visit. A good variety of species should be seen including relatively common ones like Greenfinch, Goldfinch, Linnet, Reed Bunting and Meadow Pipit. Skylarks are often seen towering above the site. In the Gorse, Stonechat appear to be taking over from Whinchat, the latter being rare at this site nowadays. Another bird that used to be commonly seen here was the Yellowhammer but it also appears to have gone from the area. Check the dry stone walls around the farm. This is where Redstarts can sometimes be seen. In the area behind the farm there is a small pond where Swallows and martins are often seen collecting mud for their nests. Continue walking as far as the Oak wood where Redstarts and Spotted Flycatchers are again possible. Pied Flycatchers once nested here but have not done so for a long time. Cuckoos are sometimes seen, presumably laying in Meadow Pipit nests.

Autumn is a good time to look for passage migrants. Early in the season family parties of woodland breeders such as Redstarts and Spotted Flycatchers can be seen feeding up prior to going on their long migrations. A Wryneck was seen in August 2004. Ever present in this area are larger birds such as Buzzard and Raven. Tawny Owls are often heard at dusk.

By going left from the car park or by back-tracking down the hill, one enters the coniferous woodland habitat of Wern Ddu. Woodcock are found in the damper areas. They have been observed roding over the area in past years. An unlikely bird to be found here is the Mallard. They frequent the weedy ponds and wetter areas on the edge of the wood. Keep an eye (and ear) out for Tree Pipit singing from the tree-tops. The area to the west of Rudry Common used to be a good spot for Nightjar. This species generally prefers young conifer plantations and as the trees have now grown, they appear to have moved on. There is a large clearing further into the woods that looks promising however.

10 - PARC CEFN ONN (ST 1884)

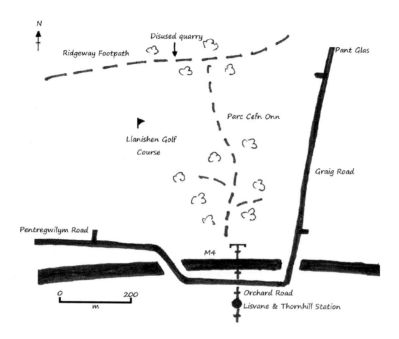

Access

Although this site is in the Cardiff UA, it has more in common with the Caerphilly Ridgeway sites than those in Cardiff, hence its inclusion in this section.

Parc Cefn Onn lies just to the north of the M4 and consists of open farmland, hedgerows, two large disused quarries, mixed woodland and wet meadow. The Ridgeway Path runs through the site. To get there from Cardiff, take the Caerphilly Mountain road (A469) past Thornhill Crematorium. The park is signposted just after the Pentre Gwilym House pub. From Caerphilly, take the mountain road past the Traveller's Rest pub. A narrow lane (Pentregwilym Road) leads on to Cherry Orchard Road. After a couple of kilometres Parc Cefn Onn is signposted on the left. There is a large car park with facilities on site. There is wheelchair access to the park but much of the rest of the site is inaccessible. The site is easily reached by public transport, being adjacent to Lisvane and Thornhill station. Accessing the park requires use of the underpass under the M4 motorway. Taking the Ridgeway path west will take you back to Caerphilly Mountain. There is no Visitor Centre on site, however it is possible to contact the Cardiff Parks department on 02920 684000.

When to visit

Spring is probably the best time to visit, not just for birds, but also for the flowers and trees.

Parc Cefn Onn is an arboretum, best known for its spring flower displays rather than its birds. The Rhododendrons in particular, are a spectacular sight in May. Over 70 species of bird have been recorded. The site contains a good mix of woodland, streams, clearings and grassland. There are several hard surfaced paths with dirt tracks leading off into surrounding areas.

The bird species that you are likely to encounter vary with the seasons. A spring visit might yield a good selection, including Cuckoo, Raven, Marsh Tit, Crossbill and passage flycatchers. The commoner warblers may also be found in this season. In summer Buzzard, Stock Doves, Redstart and Spotted Flycatcher have been seen, as has White Wagtail. Autumn is best for Tawny Owl, finches, tits and thrushes. On one occassion Black Redstart was recorded. In winter Woodcock, Fieldfare, Redwing, Siskin, Goldcrest, Jay, Nuthatch, Treecreeper and woodpeckers are likely. Although extremely scarce, Hawfinches are possible. This extremely secretive species is thought to disperse along the Caerphilly Ridgeway in the autumn.

Just to the north of the site, alongside the Ridgeway path, at ST 173853, is a disused quarry, that is worthy of exploration. It has stands of Oak, Birch, Hazel, Ash and Hawthorn growing beneath a canopy of Beech. The quarry has much floral interest. For example Autumn Gentians can be found in flower in August and September and in the spring there is a carpet of Bluebells. Lady's Mantle, Thyme and Eyebright also grow here. The bird species that have been seen here include Whitethroat, Blackcap, Redstart, Stock Dove and Raven. From August onwards there are fungi like Slimy Beech Cap and Trooping Crumble Cap to be seen. Adders and Grass Snakes may be seen basking in the unvegetated areas of the quarry. From the top of the ridge, on a clear day, there are spectacular views across the Bristol Channel to Somerset.

11 – CAERPHILLY RIDGEWAY
Coed Coesau Whips (ST 1985) and Coed Craig Ruperra (ST 2286)

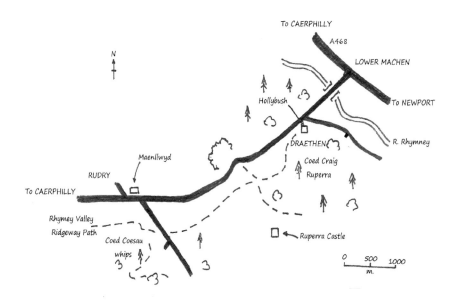

Access
These forested areas lie some 2 kilometres north of the M4, to the south of Rudry and Draethen. Both can be accessed from the A468 Caerphilly to Newport Road. Alternatively they can be reached from the minor road from Caerphilly to Rudry/Draethen. They may also be found off the minor road from Lisvane to Rudry/Draethen, which runs under the motorway.

For Coed Coesau, there is a left turn off the minor road into a small car park about 100 metres before a sharp right turn, that leads eventually to Cardiff Gate via some narrow lanes. For Ruperra, take a right turn at the Hollybush Inn in Draethen and take the left fork towards Michaelstone. The main entrance to the site is about 1 kilometre on the right hand side. The Rhymney Valley Ridgeway Path passes through both sites. Neither site has any facilities and wheelchair use would be difficult.

When to visit
Spring/early summer is best.

Coed Coesau is a very pleasant woodland area providing good views of both the Draethen Valley and Cardiff. From the car park a track bears right then left, through tall conifers, until it reaches the open areas with the most birding interest. At the northern end of the second clearing it is possible to join the Ridgeway Path by means of a steep climb up a muddy trail. Spring and early summer can bring Tree Pipits, Garden Warblers, Redstarts and Spotted Flycatchers plus some of the commoner visitors. The habitat looked suitable for Nightjar in 2006 but will become less so as the conifers grow. Winter is quieter but could be enlivened by a Buzzard/Raven dispute and one might see species such as Siskin, Redpoll and Bullfinch. Willow Tit may be just hanging on as a breeding resident.

Coed Ruperra is an ancient woodland which dates back to 1600. In the 1920's much of the site was planted with conifers. The whole area was becoming quite overgrown and unmanaged. In 2000 the Ruperra Conservation Trust took over the management of the site and have considerably improved it from a wildlife viewpoint by replacing conifers with native species. Many common woodland species can be seen here. UK Biodiversity Action Plan Priority Species found here are Song Thrush, Bullfinch, Linnet and Spotted Flycatcher. The site has been monitored as part of a BTO ringing project. In all, over 40 species have been ringed. The diversity of the site can be highlighted by examining the ringing records. These have included Blackcap, Brambling, Firecrest, Garden Warbler, Grasshopper Warbler, Redpoll, Pied Flycatcher, Redstart, Redwing, Siskin, Spotted Flycatcher, Tree Pipit, Common and Lesser Whitethroat, Willow Tit and Wood Warbler.

Redstart – Richard Morgan

12 - PARC CWM DARRAN (SO 1103)

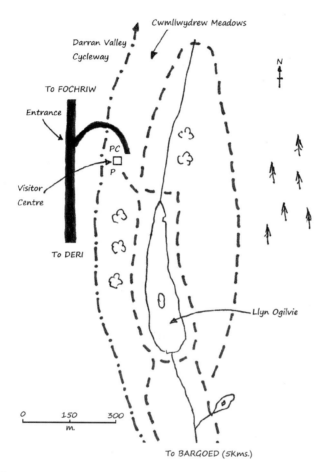

Access

From the south, follow the A469 through Bargoed. The park is signposted with brown tourist signs. Pass through the villages of Groesfaen and Deri and the entrance to the park is about a kilometre north. Take care as it is easy to miss the entrance. The road drops steeply down to the Visitor Centre.

From the north, take the A469 south to Pontlottyn and follow the brown tourist signs. There is a large car park beyond the Visitor Centre. The paths around the site are well maintained and wheelchair access is very good. More paths are under construction which clearly will be accessible for wheelchairs. The forest trails above the lakes are not. There are good facilities in the Visitor Centre although the centre and toilets are not open all year round. Call 01443 875557 to check on opening times.

When to visit
    Any time of year.

    Parc Cwm Darran was built on the site of the former Ogilvie colliery. The area has been landscaped with a large lake, grassy areas, woodland etc. There are three waymarked trails, plus numerous other paths. A cycle way also passes through the site. The majority of the site is flat and easy to negotiate. Maps of the park can be obtained from the Visitor Centre or one can refer to the main display board.

    Check the feeders around the Visitor Centre. They attract a good variety of woodland birds. Nuthatch, Long-tailed Tit and Coal Tit are all regular. A walk around Ogilvie Lake should afford views of Little Grebe, Moorhen, Coot and Mallard. Dipper and Grey Wagtail are fairly common on the stream and Kingfisher are sometimes seen. Water Rail have been seen on the island in the lake. Snipe often frequent the boggy areas on the site and Jack Snipe occasionally over-winter here. Grey Heron are quite common in the damp meadows to the north of the Visitor Centre. In the winter of 2007 a Long-tailed Duck was a surprise visitor to the lake.

    Scan the hills for raptors. Buzzard and Sparrowhawk are both quite common, whilst Red Kite are now fairly regular. Goshawk and Kestrel are not particularly common here but they occur occasionally. Raven are quite numerous, their cronking calls giving away their presence. In winter Crossbill have been seen in the conifers on the eastern slopes and both Siskin and Redpoll have been recorded.

    The wooded areas to the north of the Centre are worth checking in the spring. They can be good for both Pied and Spotted Flycatchers, although in common with elsewhere in Glamorgan these species are in decline. Wood Warblers are also possible here whilst Tree Pipits and Cuckoo may be seen in the clearings. All three woodpeckers can be found here, as can Tawny Owl.

    Many birders combine a visit to the park with a visit to nearby Fochrhiw Reservoir (SS 099055).

13 – NELSON
Nelson Wern (ST 1195) and Parc Penallta (ST 1295)

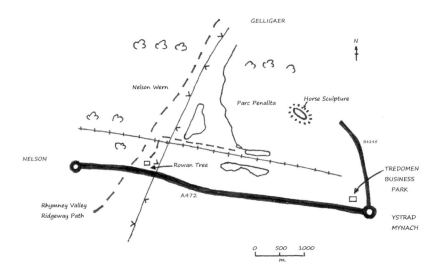

Access
  Nelson Wern lies alongside the A472 Ystrad Mynach to Nelson road. Cars can be parked next to the roundabout, just before entering Nelson. A tarmac path follows the railway line towards Parc Penallta. (This path is part of the National Cycle Network) Much of the site has been reclaimed from coal spoil and it is maturing rapidly. It is not advisable to leave the footpaths, as there are some deep areas. Boots or wellingtons are recommended. Wheelchair access is possible at both sites, although it would be very awkward getting over the railway line. Work is under way to correct this. It would be impossible to use the grass paths. The phone number for Parc Penallta is 01443 816853.

When to visit
  Can be productive at any time of year.

  The Wern is managed with wildlife in mind and has meadows with orchids and butterflies in abundance. Some of the trees have been deliberately ring-barked in order to kill them. With luck, as they rot they will encourage woodpeckers. All three species are seen in the Park. The path between the boardwalk and the railway is good for Willow Tit and the man-made scrapes can hold Kingfishers. Early morning visits are recommended before the birds are disturbed. During the winter, the railway crossing is a good spot for both Siskin and Redpoll.

After crossing the railway line, go over the style. This part of the path can be a little overgrown but after a 50 metre scramble, it opens up into fields. After crossing two more styles, there is a choice of route. The first runs diagonally up the field to an area of mature woodland that contains most of the expected species, including the now locally scarce Wood Warbler. A walk through the woods eventually leads into Parc Penallta. By turning right towards the main pond there is a good chance of seeing Reed Warblers, as the reeds here are not too dense.

Reed Warbler – Bob Mitchell

Alternatively, after the second style, turn right along the edge of the woods, through a gate and up a small rise. From here there is an excellent view of Nelson Bog SSSI, with Reed Warblers in abundance and a good chance of glimpsing Water Rail. A little further on there is a stone railway bridge. Follow the path and turn right to return to Nelson Wern or left to access Parc Penallta. Goldcrest and Bullfinch may be found along the cycle path. In winter there are often Redwing and Fieldfare feeding on the berry-bearing bushes. Several raptor species can be seen over the park with Buzzard being relatively common. Hobby may be seen in late summer, hunting the Swallows and martins as they gather for their long migratory journey to Africa.

Parc Penallta is also an excellent place to see dragonflies and on a good day 15 species may be found. There are many paths around this country park and it is worthy of exploration. The site maps show three colour coded trails. For the main access point to Parc Penallta, leave the A472 at the Tredomen Business Park and follow the B4245 towards Gelligaer. There are brown tourist signs indicating the park. The entrance to the park is on your left. There is plenty of car parking space.

Caerphilly Borough Council runs guided bird walks. Contact Dave Beveridge on 01495 235464 or beverd@caerphilly.gov.uk

Area 3 : CARDIFF

Site 14 Cardiff Bay
Site 15 Cardiff Foreshore
Site 16 Lamby Lake
Site 17 Bute Park
Site 18 Hendre Lake
Site 19 Llanishen/Lisvane Reservoirs
Site 20 Roath Park Lake
Site 21 Coed-y-Bedw and the Garth
Site 22 Forest Farm and Glamorgan Canal
Site 23 Tongwynlais

Dunlin – Bob Mitchell

14 - CARDIFF BAY (ST 1873)

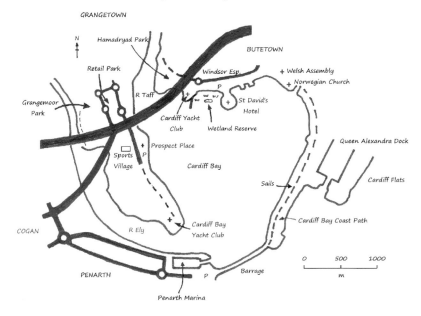

Access

The Cardiff Bay Development Corporation was founded in 1987 with the aim of regenerating over 1100 hectares of derelict docklands. Part of the plan was to build a barrage across the mouth of the Rivers Taff and Ely. The barrage was completed in 1999, thus converting the area from tidal mudflats into a permanent fresh water lake. There was much concern at the time, as the mudflats had SSSI status. The lake that was created is 500 hectares in area and has a waterfront of approximately 12 kilometres. Some compensatory measures, such as the Cardiff Bay Wetlands Reserve, were put into place to maintain some of the wildlife interest in the bay (The Gwent Wetlands Reserve was also created as compensation for the loss of habitat in the bay)

The lake now holds a variety of bird species, albeit not necessarily the ones that were there before the building of the barrage. There are several access points. The Wetland Reserve is accessed from Windsor Esplanade, where parking is free (if you can find a space). Coming from the bay bridge on the A4232, take the slip road signposted 'Techniquest', just before the tunnels and turn right at the roundabout. From Cardiff Bay/Mermaid Quay, go along

45

Stuart Street then turn left into Dudley Street, off the roundabout at the start of the slip road down to the A4232. Turn right at the far end. If there isn't any room, try the pay and display car park behind Techniquest.

Alternatively, you can view the bay from the barrage. Park in the pay and display car park at the end of the Penarth Marina development. Both sites are accessible for wheelchair users. There are plenty of facilities available in the area. The whole of the bay is undergoing rapid development and as a consequence, viewing areas and access points are likely to change in the future.

When to visit

This site is worth a visit at any time of year, although the summer can be quiet.

A good starting point is the Cardiff Bay Wetland Reserve. Walk along the boardwalk that runs through the reserve and scan the marsh and shallow lagoons for duck and waders. In winter, good numbers of Teal, Tufted Duck and Snipe can be found here. Grey Heron and Little Egret are also possible. Gulls often rest on the buoys. As well as the commoner species, Mediterranean, Little, Ring-billed, Glaucous, and Bonaparte's have all been recorded. Check the channel alongside the St. David's Hotel for Kingfishers. Lapwings are regularly found in the scrape in front of the hotel. Other duck that might possibly be seen in winter are Scaup, Goldeneye, Gadwall and occasionally Shelduck. An American Wigeon was here in April 2006 and a Lesser Scaup graced the reserve in January 2009. Reed Buntings are sometimes present in the vegetated area and in March 2007 four Bearded Tits were found in the reedy area.

Whilst in this area it is worthwhile checking Hamadryad Park. This is a landscaped park with grassy areas and trees. A limited number of passerines can be found here. A recommended walk is via the path that skirts the River Taff. Gulls, Cormorants and Herons often rest here and Dipper and Kingfisher have both been recorded.

Elsewhere, around Prospect Place, you should encounter good numbers of Great Crested Grebes. A Slavonian Grebe was a long stayer in December 2008. Currently the best place to view is from the boardwalk that runs from the Sports Village to the Cardiff Bay Yacht Club (a different club from that next to the Wetland Reserve). Note that development work is continuing in this area.

Nearby 'Grangemoor Park', a man-made hill between Cardiff Bay Retail Park and the River Ely can be worth a visit. Birds include Reed Buntings, a variety of finches, Kestrel, Skylarks and Meadow Pipits. Wheatears are often recorded on passage. To inspect the River Ely, take the gravel path that runs alongside.

On the other side of the bay, the barrage can host some 'good' birds. Amongst the common passerines likely to be seen are Linnet, Pied Wagtails, Stonechat, Meadow and Rock Pipits. Check out the rough ground at the eastern end of the barrage as in winter, as Black Redstarts may be found there. Rarer individuals that have been seen are Snow Bunting and Dartford Warbler. Don't ignore the rocks on the seaward side of the barrage, as waders such as Oystercatchers may occur. It is always amusing to watch the Cormorants fishing alongside the sluice gates, as they dive into the surf. If you have a telescope, check the bay for species such as Goosander, Long-tailed Duck and grebe species. Gull watching may prove fruitful. Recently, a Ring-billed Gull has had the habit of perching on the railings at the exit to the Penarth Marina. On passage, terns may also be seen in the bay and in spring, hirundines are attracted to the lake. Large numbers of Swifts can be seen on their autumn passage, as they 'hawk' for insects over the bay. This occurs in poor weather when their insect prey is flying low. It is now possible to walk around the whole bay as the coastal path across the barrage was opened in June 2008.

Lesser-black Backed Gull – Alan Rosney

15 – CARDIFF FORESHORE

Rhymney Estuary (ST 2277), Cors Crychydd Reen (ST 2278)
Rumney Great Wharf (ST 2377), Water Treatment Works (ST 2175)
and the Heliport (ST 2174)

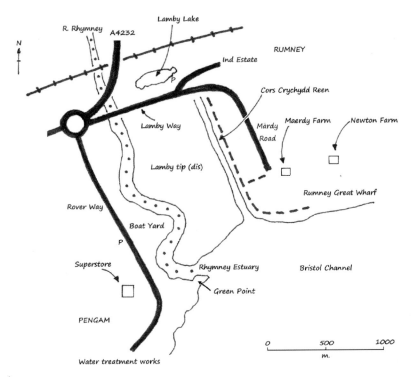

Access

The best access is via Rover Way. This road can be very busy
with lorries and other heavy traffic, although it is generally a lot
quieter on Sundays. There is a Tesco Extra superstore on Rover Way,
where there is ample parking (if done discretely). Enter at the traffic
lights and park in the corner nearest Rover Way and the lights,
(avoid the commercial vehicle lane next to Rover Way). This is a
long way from the store entrance and is rarely used. The only public
facilities are in Tesco Extra. Much of the site is very wet so
wellingtons are recommended. Wheelchair users cannot access much
of the estuary.

The whole area has great potential for bird watching. Two other sites in the locality, Cors Crychydd Reen and Rumney Great Wharf are also worthy of investigation. The entrance to the reen is 200 metres east of the landfill roundabout. Entry is via a metal barrier. The best place to park is in the car park at Lamby Lake. There are no public facilities in the area. The barriers at the entrance to the reen would make wheelchair access difficult; however access is possible from Mardy Road. To get on to Rumney Great Wharf, turn left (east), over a rocky stile at the seaward end of the reen. This leads on to the sea wall which overlooks the Wharf. Try not to break the skyline as the birds are easily disturbed in this area

When to visit

This site is most productive in winter, although it deserves attention in spring and autumn too.

The main attractions in the winter are undoubtedly wildfowl, waders and gulls. The best time to visit is near the 'top' of the tide (rising or falling) as many birds are forced up on to the banks of the estuary.

To explore the estuary it is probably best to use the boatyard entrance on Rover Way. Turn right, cross over an earth bank, and follow the path adjacent to the road. There is often fly-tipping here. In spring, autumn and winter check the trees and scrub alongside the boatyard for passerines.

Further along, the river comes in to view. Teal are usually the first duck to be seen in the river or on the banks. Check the scrub on the left for Stonechat and warblers like Whitethroat. After a 'metalled' section of path there are some reeds on the left, plus a small stand of trees. There are gaps you can pass through (this area is sometimes quite wet at high tide) on to the flat area where the river loops round to its mouth. This area is often called Green Point by the locals. It is composed mainly of long wet grass, with a ditch running across, which can be crossed at various points. Approach carefully as the waders often roost on the left hand river bank. Redshank are usually the main waders present (up to 900 have been recorded). Dunlin and Knot are also frequently seen. Curlew, Whimbrel and both godwits are occasional visitors whilst Ruff and Spotted Redshank are less frequent. Undoubtedly the rarest wader encountered was a Long-billed Dowitcher that was found in March 1989. This is the only occurrence of this species in Glamorgan to date.

Shelduck often roost on the rocky promontory at the far end of Green Point. There is a small reed bed to the right, which unfortunately has reduced in size recently as a result of fly tipping but it is still worth checking. Jack Snipe are regular here in winter, typically flushing from the shallow pools in the immediate vicinity of the reeds. Common Snipe might also be present.

Offshore, the duck are best viewed from higher ground with a telescope. Shelduck are always present in winter (up to 700) together with Pintail. Numbers are however lower than in the past, with only 300 being recorded recently. Also regular are smaller numbers of Teal, Wigeon and Shoveler, plus occasional Pochard, Scaup, Tufted Duck. Brent Goose and Mute Swan have also been observed. Ringed Plover, Turnstone and Oystercatcher can often be found on the beach here but are easily flushed. Large numbers of waders may gather on the beach opposite Green Point however a telescope is essential to view them. Gulls are ever present in large numbers due to the adjacent landfill site. Glaucous, Iceland and Mediterranean have all been recorded. Peregrine and Merlin are possible in winter - for the former, check the pylons. The upstream section of the river is best checked from the road. Redshank often roost here. Walk back along the road from the Lamby Lake car park. This road is very busy and is used by heavy lorries.

Cors Crychydd Reen has breeding Little Grebe, Coot, Moorhen and Mute Swan with small numbers of Reed and Sedge Warblers. Check the bramble and scrub area for Cetti's Warblers and Whitethroats. In winter, Green Sandpipers often get into the small side reen which runs from the bridge at the far end. Barn Owl might be seen in this area too. In winter, thrushes can be present. Grey Heron and Little Egret are occasional visitors and a real rarity, a Squacco Heron, paid a brief visit in June 2003.

About halfway along Cors Crychydd Reen, a path leads off east to Mardy Road. Turn left and walk down the road (north) until you reach a dirt lay-by on the left. In the middle of the field on the opposite side of the road is a large Oak with two holes in its trunk. If you are lucky Little and Barn Owls might be seen here. There are a couple of places where there are gaps through the hedgerow to view the tree. **[Please do not enter the field, as it is private property].**

This area can be reached by driving down Mardy Road from Wentloog Road. Nearby Newton Farm caravan site is worthy of investigation as it is used by roosting gulls. The drainage ditches can also be productive with Snipe and Green Sandpiper being possible.

At the seaward end of the reen there is a small pool behind the sea wall. This marks the beginning of Rumney Great Wharf. Walking to the west leads round to a point overlooking the river mouth. Take care not to break the skyline as you may flush resting birds. Rumney Great Wharf is a good area for roosting waders at high tide. It is often worthwhile scanning eastwards towards the distant groyne. Good numbers of wildfowl can be offshore and in the right conditions (south-westerly blow), sea-watching can be productive. Scoter, terns and skuas have been seen. It is possible to walk all the way along the sea wall as far as Sluice Farm (Gwent), although there is a somewhat overgrown stretch after about 3-400 metres. The whole foreshore is worth checking for spring and autumn migrants. Look for Wheatear and Yellow Wagtail on the broader rocky foreshore near the border with Gwent, as well as on the rocky 'finger' opposite the trig. point on the sea wall at end of the reen. Short-eared Owls have been observed here in winter and Kingfishers are occasionally seen, as are commoner species such as Stonechat.

Two further sites to the west of the estuary are the Water Treatment Works (ST 2275) and Cardiff Heliport (ST 2174). **[Re-development here means that access is in a state of flux. As a consequence no site maps have been provided for these sites].**

The Water Treatment Works are signposted off the roundabout on Rover Way, as the road passes in front of Tremorfa Steel Works. In the past it was possible to access the Cardiff East foreshore and the old landscaped Tremorfa tip via the car park next to the Treatment Works entrance but serious fly-tipping has caused the entrance to be locked. There are plans to turn this area into parkland in future and the All Wales coastal path is scheduled to pass through the area. The lagoons and structures of the WTW attract thousands of gulls and Sabine's Gull has been recorded.

The Heliport site can be accessed from the Cardiff end of Rover Way. There is a small roundabout that provides access to Cardiff East docks. Take the docks exit, drive for 100 metres and turn left into the industrial estate. Turn left at the first opportunity and follow the road round a right hand bend, parking at the far end, just as it turns left.

This site has been completely re-developed in recent years. The two fields that used to exist here were very productive but unfortunately they are now under industrial units. However, the so-called Heliport Bay and the Bristol Channel can still be observed. It is possible to walk between the industrial units and over the bank that overlooks Heliport Bay. The bay itself used to have reasonable numbers of waders at high tide but does not seem to be as productive nowadays, possibly as a result of the impoundment of the Taff/Ely. The rocky foreshore can hold a small flock of Turnstone, sometimes with attendant Ringed Plovers. By walking seawards along the sea wall, a good view of the Bristol Channel can be obtained. Sea-watching from either the WTW or the Heliport can be profitable, especially after westerly storms in spring and autumn. Whilst gulls are certain to dominate, there have been sightings of rare birds such as skuas, particularly Pomarines. Other sea birds that have been encountered include Manx Shearwater and Gannet.

Sandwich Tern – Paul Parsons

16 - LAMBY LAKE (ST 2178)
This site is also known as Parc Tredelerch

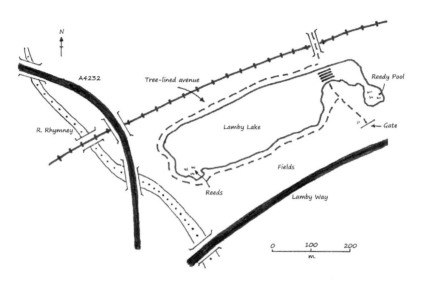

Access
Turn off the M4 at Junction 30. Connect with the A48 and follow the signs for the docks. Turn left into Lamby Way at the first roundabout (just after the flyover). The entrance is on your left alongside the next roundabout. There are plenty of car parking spaces. The footpaths are well surfaced and suitable for wheelchair use. The car park here can also be used for accessing Cors Crychydd Reen (See the Cardiff foreshore site guide).

When to visit
It can be productive at any time of year.

Lamby Lake or Parc Tredelerch, is a relatively new site, having only been created in 2001. The site is becoming more attractive season by season.

There is a main fishing lake connected with a smaller pond by a short ditch and a long reen. There are also a few reedy water-filled hollows which are worth checking. A well maintained path goes right round the perimeter of the lake and a tree-lined avenue runs parallel with the northern edge. Sedges, small shrubs and marshy grass cover much of the open land to the south. To the west lies the River Rhymney, where many waders and gulls congregate.

A variety of birds can be seen at any time of year, including Grey Wagtail, Stonechat, Reed Bunting, Goldcrest, Meadow Pipit, Snipe, Buzzard, Kestrel, Raven, Great Crested Grebe, Little Grebe, Grey Heron, Shelduck, Lapwing, Redshank plus finches and tits. Early mornings may produce Little Egret and Water Rail.

Winter can bring plenty of wildfowl. Tufted Duck, Pochard, Goldeneye and Teal are the most likely species. Gadwall tend to appear later in the season. The scrub area behind the tree-lined avenue can hold a number of species. You might encounter Fieldfare, Redwing, Mistle Thrush, Redpoll and Siskin. Over-wintering Chiffchaffs and Blackcaps may also be found. Both Jack Snipe and Green Sandpiper occasionally over-winter. Birds of prey, including Merlin and Peregrine, may also be seen here in the winter season.

Summer brings breeding migrants and the reeds come alive with the sound of Reed and Sedge Warblers. Willow Warbler, Chiffchaff, Blackcap, Whitethroat and Lesser Whitethroat can be found in the tree-lined avenue. Swifts, Swallows, Sand and House Martins may be seen feeding over the lake and Skylarks can often be observed hovering over the open ground. Pipits and wagtails are also likely here. Lesser Black-backed Gulls come to the lake in summer and both Common and Herring Gulls also visit regularly.

Common and Green Sandpipers may be seen on passage, as can Wheatear, Whinchat and Spotted Flycatcher. It is best to search for these early in the morning, before the site is disturbed by dog walkers, fishermen etc.

Despite being a relatively 'new' site, it has hosted some scarce birds. Its position close to the coast is obviously a factor. Famously, a Squacco Heron was here in June 2003, being only the third for the recording area. Also seen in 2003 were Bearded Tit, Garganey and even a Red-throated Diver. Other scarce birds that have been recorded are Hobby, Ring-billed, Yellow-legged and Bonaparte's Gulls, Red-legged Partridge, Marsh Tit, Tree Sparrow and Slavonian Grebe. In January 2009, there were two Ring-billed Gulls, which proved popular with photographers.

17 - BUTE PARK (ST 1777)

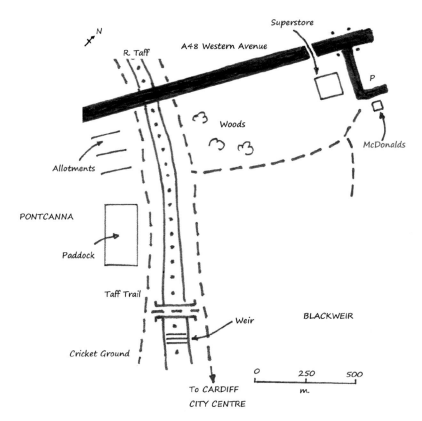

Access

Bute Park lies in the very heart of Cardiff. It stretches all the way from the rear of Cardiff Castle right up to the Western Avenue Bridge. The best birding area is undoubtedly at the northern end, near Western Avenue Bridge. The park has a mix of landscaped woodland/parkland running alongside the River Taff. To the west of the park are playing fields that can be attractive for birds. The paths are well maintained and accessible for wheelchairs. The park was set up by the Marques of Bute and was presented to the city in 1947. It has mature trees, grassland and flowerbeds. The Taff Trail links this area with sites further north. Japanese Knotweed, the scourge of rivers in South Wales, is encroaching along the river banks.

There are many access points; three of which are described:

1. From Western Avenue, there are paths either side of the river.
2. From the City Centre, go through the park gates on Cardiff Bridge and walk through Coopers Field or park in the Sophia Gardens car park and cross the river via the footbridge.
3. From North Road, access the park at Blackweir.

When to visit
Any time of year - a haven of peace in a busy city.

The park contains many common species such as tits, finches, and thrushes. In spring, Chiffchaff can be heard and the call of the Nuthatch often rings out. Chiffchaff are increasingly over-wintering. Jays and woodpeckers can often be seen in the wooded areas. Green Woodpeckers and Mistle Thrushes, in particular, seem to enjoy the manicured grassy areas of the park.

The reason why many bird watchers visit the park is to try and see Lesser Spotted Woodpecker. They have been seen regularly in the area by the Horse Paddocks, opposite Pontcanna fields. A spring visit, before the leaves are on the trees may be rewarded. With luck their call will alert you to their presence.

.   The park hosted a flock of Waxwings during the unprecedented invasion in 2004/5. They were making short work of the berries on the ornamental Rowan trees behind the College of Music building. In recent winters, a Firecrest has over-wintered in the riverside bushes close to the Western Avenue bridge and on one occasion it was joined by a Yellow-browed Warbler.

As well as Black-headed Gulls and Mallard, the river often has Goosander in winter. Good views can be had from the footbridge. A flash of blue might alert one to the presence of a Kingfisher. This species seems to be increasing in numbers recently. Dippers are often seen on the rocks near the Western Avenue Bridge and both Grey and Pied Wagtails can be seen on the river banks.

The sports fields of Pontcanna can hold significant numbers of thrushes which feed on the short turf. They are often joined by parties of corvids. A short stroll from the park will take you into the Civic Centre. It may be worth checking the City Hall clock tower; as Raven and Peregrine have nested there in recent years.

18 - HENDRE LAKE (ST 2480)

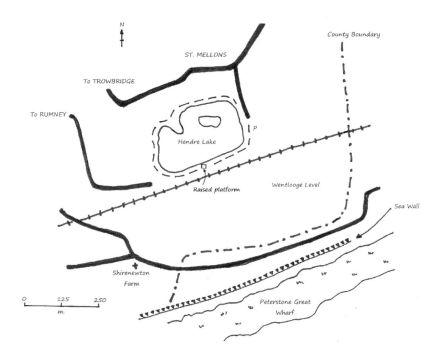

Access

This small lake is located at the eastern end of Cardiff, adjacent to and north of the main London - South Wales railway line. It is reached by turning south of the A48 into Cypress Drive, at the large roundabout to the east of St Mellons village. A car park is provided at the end of Cypress Drive, although it is rather poorly maintained. The lake is popular with both local fishermen and dog walkers but nevertheless it retains some ornithological interest. Parts of the site can be quite boggy and wellingtons are recommended. Wheelchair access is possible along the paths.

When to visit

It can be productive at any time of year.

The bird list of this site is not particularly large. It is primarily used as a fishing lake. However there are a number of breeding species These include Great Crested Grebe, Mute Swan, Canada Goose, Moorhen, Coot and Mallard. Breeding warblers include Reed, Sedge, Whitethroat and Lesser Whitethroat. Cetti's Warbler has been recorded recently but has not yet bred.

Winter usually brings a few Snipe, when the nearby fields are flooded. There is also the possibility of encountering the smaller Jack Snipe at this time. Other waders also occur, including Green Sandpipers which sometimes winter nearby. Grey Heron, Kingfisher and Little Egret often visit the lake Some scarce birds, such as Slavonian Grebe, Red Breasted Merganser and Goosander have been recorded but as is typical, their visits are usually very brief.

Pied Wagtail – Alan Rosney

As the site is only a short distance from the coast, passage migrants occasionally drop in. The area is a stop-over and re-fuelling point for these passage migrants. Goldfinch numbers for example, often reach three figures during the autumn passage period, though there are few present during the rest of the year. Many other relatively common species can also be seen passing through. Whilst the appearance of scarcities is as ever, unpredictable. Hen Harrier, Hobby, Little Ringed Plover, Bittern, Ruff, Little Tern, Black Tern, Turtle Dove, Black Redstart, Grasshopper Warbler and Hawfinch have all been recorded.

19 – LLANISHEN AND LISVANE RESERVOIRS
Llanishen (ST 1882), Lisvane (ST 1881)

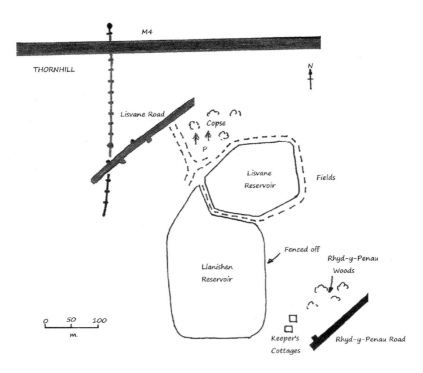

Access

Lying 4-5 kilometres north of Cardiff city centre, these two reservoirs can provide some good bird watching in a relatively built up area. They are not particularly easy to find however. From the M4, go south from Junction 32 (Coryton) towards Cardiff on the A470, Northern Avenue. At the second set of traffic lights turn left on to Tyn y Parc Road. Stay on this road until the second set of traffic lights and turn left again, going north towards Caerphilly on the A469. At the roundabout, turn right towards Lisvane, then at the second set of traffic lights bear left. From the next roundabout, take the second exit along Ty-Glas Road into the village. At the next junction give way to traffic from the right before turning on to Station/Lisvane Road. Carry on this road over the railway bridge hump on Mill Road. On the left is a white house. Keep straight on for another 100 metres and the narrow entrance is on your right. It is very easy to miss.

59

There are two car parks, one at the Lisvane Road entrance, with another at the Rhyd-y-Penau entrance. There are toilets near both entrances. In the past the site was wardened, however there has not been a warden on site for some time. There has been a long-running disagreement over the future of the site. The reservoirs are now redundant and developers have targetted the site. It is still not clear what the future holds. The discovery of several species of Waxcaps, notably the Pink Waxcap (Hygrocybe calyptriformis), a UK Biodiversity Action Plan species, has halted development for the time being. Recently Llanishen Reservoir has been fenced off, making viewing difficult. The Lisvane site is designated as an SSSI and is the better of the two reservoirs for bird watching. There are grassy footpaths, which can get quite muddy. Wheelchair users should be able to scan from the car park. Early morning is best, as dog walkers tend to disturb the birds later on.

When to visit
Winter is usually the best season to visit. Spring and autumn passage can bring surprises.

For bird watching it is probably best to walk from the Lisvane entrance. The belt of conifers near the entrance is always worth checking. Evergreen specialists such as Goldcrest, Siskin and Coal Tit are often seen here. From the car park turn left and take the path around the edge of the reservoir. On the left there are deciduous trees which host many of the commoner woodland specialities. It is worth checking this area for migrants at passage times. Of the resident birds, woodpeckers are present, including the extremely elusive Lesser Spotted. Tawny Owls are also resident in these woods. On the right, the main area of interest is of course the reservoir. It is possible to scan the water with binoculars, although a telescope is recommended. The commoner duck species include Mallard, Pochard and Tufted Duck. In winter, Gadwall, Goldeneye and Shoveler can be seen. If you are lucky, Goosander may be present. Sometimes the unexpected turns up. For example, the 'Kenfig' Redhead made an appearance in February 2003 and a there was a storm driven Gannet in March 2006. Little Grebes are often quite numerous on Lisvane and Great Crested Grebes are often present. Rarer grebes and divers have been recorded e.g. in April 2006 there were three Black-necked Grebes, presumably the same birds that over-wintered on Ynysfro Reservoir in Gwent.

Black-necked Grebe – Bob Mitchell

The seemingly uninviting masonry walls are worth checking. The sides have regularly attracted passage waders, especially if water levels are low. Common Sandpiper is the most regular, however in October 2007, a juvenile Spotted Sandpiper was a surprise find. It proved to be a very popular bird, attracting many birders to the site. It was extremely tame and provided good photo opportunities. It stayed well into 2008. Wagtails, both Pied and Grey, may also be found on the reservoir sides. In summer hirundines hunt insects over the water. This is quite a reliable site for Sand Martins which pass through in March. As you reach the far end of the reservoir there is a Hawthorn hedgerow that can prove attractive for warblers. Particularly on a sunny day in September, you might see Willow Warblers, Chiffchaffs and Blackcaps working their way along the hedgerow. In winter the hedgerow fruits also attract Redwing and Fieldfare. Don't ignore the skies as Buzzard, Sparrowhawk and Goshawk are possibilities. Hobby is a scarce but regular summer visitor that hunts Swallows and martins over the reservoirs

Next to Lisvane is the larger Llanishen Reservoir. It is less productive than Lisvane. Being deeper, it tends to attract fewer species and gulls tend to predominate. It tends to suffer from disturbance from the yachts that use the lake and the fishermen don't take kindly to the Cormorants that frequent the site. Once again some rare divers, ducks and grebes have been observed notably Black-throated Diver, Long-tailed Duck and Red-necked Grebe.

20 - ROATH PARK LAKE (ST 1879)

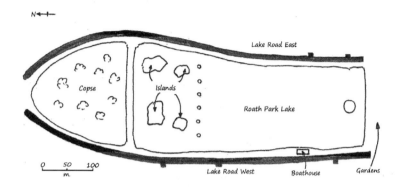

Access

Roath Park Lake lies about 3 kilometres from Cardiff City centre. It is approximately 700 by 100 metres and is large enough to feature on City maps. It is not on any of the main routes but is flanked by Cyncoed Road to the east and Allensbank Road to the west. Turning left or right respectively from these roads will lead to Lake Road East or West. It is a multi-purpose facility with fishing and boating on the lake. Walkers and joggers use the paths around the lake. Despite this, the area can be productive for bird watching. A stroll right around the lake should take about an hour. Parking is easy around the lake, especially at the north end and the area is well served by public transport. There are toilets in the gardens at the southern end. The cafeteria is open in the summer months. Wheelchair access is excellent all around the lake.

When to visit

Any time of year although summer can be quiet. Early morning is recommended.

The lake is known primarily for its waterfowl and gulls. The close proximity to Llanishen/Lisvane Reservoirs means that birds can commute between the two sites, if disturbed at one or the other. The lake is very popular with the general public. Children often feed the pinioned ducks, which include exotic species such as Carolina Duck, Chiloe Wigeon, Mandarin and Red Crested Pochard, as well as Eider and Shoveler. Swans and geese are also present.

Although the lake provides the most interest, the wooded areas around the lake, especially at the northern end, can hold migratory species such as Chiffchaff and Blackcap. Other species that might be encountered are Great Spotted Woodpecker, Nuthatch, Grey Wagtail, Treecreeper, Tawny Owl and various tit species. The conifers may hold Goldcrest, Coal Tit and Siskin.

Gulls can be seen in all seasons, although the winter season is probably the best. Gull numbers build up from late autumn. Birds are often attracted to bread near the lake's edge. Quite significant gull numbers can gather on the lake with Black-headed, Lesser Black-backed, Herring and Common Gulls being present at various times of year. The gulls use the lake to bathe after feeding on the coast or on local refuse tips. It is therefore a good place to test out your identification skills, as they are present in various stages of moult, from juvenile to adult plumage. Rarer Gulls such as Little, Ring Billed, Iceland and Mediterranean have been seen. Wild ducks include Mallard, Pochard and Tufted Duck. Free flying Mandarins have been also been recorded. The island at the northern end of the lake provides a roosting site for Cormorant, Grey Heron and Wood Pigeon. Kingfishers can be seen here too. It was here that a Night Heron was found in November 1989.

Winter thrush flocks can gather on the berry laden bushes in the gardens at the southern end of the lake.

Canada Goose – Paul Parsons

21 - COED-Y-BEDW AND THE GARTH
Coedy-Bedw (ST 1082), The Garth (ST 1083)

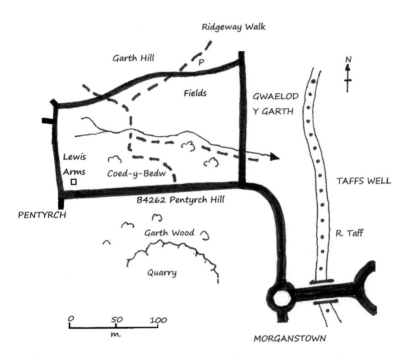

Access

This is a mixed area of open woodland and grassy slopes. The sites are reached by taking the A470 north to the Radyr/Tongwynlais exit. Cross the River Taff, at the roundabout and take the Pentyrch road. Travel up the steep hill for a few hundred metres until you see a quarry entrance on your left. Parking is problematical. It may be possible to find a spot alongside this entrance but beware as heavy lorries continually use the site. (Work is underway to create a different lorry entrance to the quarry). Cross the road and enter Coed-y-Bedw woods over the stile. Don't be tempted to use the pull-in near the top of the hill. The owners of the fields need access for their horses and generally do not take kindly to visitors. Unfortunately wheelchair access is impossible at this site. Wellingtons or walking boots are recommended.

If you merely wish to explore the Garth Mountain, it is possible to access it via Pentyrch. Just beyond the Lewis Arms, at the top of Pentyrch hill, there is a T junction. Turn right and right again. This leads on to the mountain road, where it should be possible to find a parking place. The alternative access lane via Gwaelod y Garth is extremely narrow and there are some very sharp bends to negotiate. The lay-by on this road is a common target for car thieves as are all the secluded parking places in the Garth area. There are several footpaths on the Garth, including the Ridgeway Walk. These paths can be very steep in parts.

When to visit

Spring and early summer are best.

Coed-y-Bedw is a typical Oak/Beech woodland with stands of Alder in the damper areas near the streams. There are numerous paths through the woods, some of which can prove to be a little slippery, particularly after rain. The wood is criss-crossed by small streams, most of which are bridged. The reserve has been managed by WTSWW for many years. It is a long narrow wood, stretching almost all the way from Gwaelod-y-Garth up to the village of Pentyrch. The site has long been known for its Pied Flycatchers. Numbers have plummeted recently and there are fears that they may have been lost as a breeding species. In 2007 only one female returned to the wood, consequently breeding did not take place and no birds were recorded in 2008. Wood Warbler has suffered a similar fate and is now only recorded on passage. Despite these losses the wood is still worth exploring. In spring the smell of the Wild Garlic is unforgettable and the carpet of Bluebells is a very pretty sight. The floral mix is made more interesting because of the fact that the springs in the south-west of the reserve are lime-rich, whilst the main stream, the Nant Cwmllwydrew, is acidic. Along this stream, rare Giant Lacewings can be found in early summer. The site also has a decent butterfly list. Numbers appear to be in decline, however Silver-washed Fritillary, Dark Green Fritillary and Purple Hairstreak have all being recorded in the past. Butterfly enthusiasts might wish to explore the sunny south-facing slopes of the Garth Mountain. Small Pearl-bordered Fritillaries have been seen here.

Common woodland species should be seen. Woodpeckers are relatively numerous, including occasional sightings of Lesser Spotted. Green Woodpeckers favour the grassy glades at the foot of the slope, where they forage on the anthills of the Yellow Ant. Both Blackcap and Chiffchaff are breeding species and Willow Warblers are sometimes found at the top (western) end of the reserve. Look out for Nuthatch, Treecreeper, Goldcrest and various tit species, all of which are relatively common here. In the centre of the reserve is a small woodland pond which attracts birds. It is also worth checking for frog spawn in spring as well as damselflies and dragonflies in summer.

Crossing the stile out of the wood to explore the mountain side is particularly recommended. Several footpaths lead up to a series of isolated Oak trees. In spring, Redstart can be found in the leaf canopy and with luck Cuckoo might be heard. At the western end of the reserve, Grey Wagtails can be seen on the woodland streams and Spotted Flycatchers, although never very common, may be seen on the edge of the wood. The mountain side supports typical grassland species such as Meadow Pipit and Skylark.

Blackcap – Paul Parsons

This is a site where it can be profitable to watch the skies. Buzzards can be regularly seen soaring over the Garth Mountain and Peregrines can also be observed in the area. As well as these two, several other species of raptors have been recorded. The adjacent Taff valley appears to be a fly-way for these birds. Honey Buzzard, Osprey, Hobby and Black Kite have all been observed from here and Hen Harrier has been recorded quartering the mountain in winter. After your visit it might be worth stopping at the roundabout at the bottom of Pentyrch hill. It should be possible to park in or alongside one of the industrial/office units. By scanning from the bridge over the Taff; Dippers, Grey Wagtails, Cormorants and Grey Herons might be seen. In winter, Goosanders also use this stretch of river.

22 - FOREST FARM AND GLAMORGAN CANAL
Forest Farm (ST 1480), Glamorgan Canal (ST 1381)

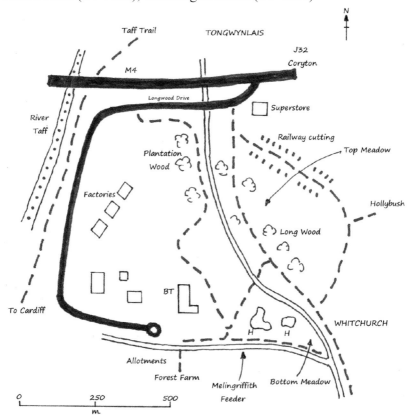

Access

This site can be easily reached by train, a tunnel and footbridge lead from Radyr Station. By car, the site may be accessed from the Coryton roundabout (Junction 32 on the M4). Take the exit for the ASDA superstore. Do not enter the superstore site but take the second exit at the roundabout. Follow the signs for Forest Farm. There is convenient roadside parking. An alternative route is from Whitchurch via Velindre Road and Forest Farm Road. The majority of the paths have hard surfaces, although they can get muddy at times. The terrain is generally flat. The exception is the upper ridge path where boots or wellingtons are necessary. The Taff Trail runs into the north of the reserve. Wheelchair users will not be able to use the upper path, although the lower paths are accessible. The nearest facilities are in the ASDA superstore.

When to visit

This site is most productive in winter.

This is a little gem (60 hectares) of a reserve. It is a haven of peace in a heavily built up area. Formerly an area of heavy industry, much of the site is now designated with SSSI status and is an LNR. There are several habitats, ranging from Oak/Beech woodland, grazed meadows, Alder Carr to water features such as the old canal. The River Taff runs down the western border of the site. The reserve stretches from the Taff at Radyr in the west to a pronounced wooded ridge below the ASDA store. Within this site are three separate water features. The River Taff, the old works (Melingriffith) feeder and one of the few remaining sections of the former Glamorganshire Canal. This 40 kilometre long canal was closed in 1942. It fell into disrepair and much of it was lost. There has been some office and industrial development in recent years but it has also seen the creation of wetland reserves between the feeder and the canal.

The upper footpath can be accessed from the rear of the ASDA car park. Go to the far end of the car park, where there is a footpath. Almost immediately left on the footpath is a small heronry, high in the trees behind the wire fence. The woods below to the right can be viewed at canopy height from the path. An alternative is to use the path that leads from the rear of McDonalds. A variety of typical woodland species occurs, including all three woodpeckers, although the elusive Lesser Spotted is rarely seen far from the canal. The footpath eventually drops down to the canal side level. The woods have a mix of interesting flora such as Wild Garlic, Bluebell and Dog Violet, whilst the flooded parts have Marsh Marigold.

Another way to access the reserve is from the end of Longwood Drive. Park carefully because the gates are in use most of the time, although less so at weekends. Follow the path with the feeder to your right, ignoring the path to the left, go through the gate and continue following the feeder. There are two gates to the left, each leading to a hide overlooking small wetlands. The first hide overlooks a small lake where Little Grebe, Water Rail, Grey Heron and Kingfisher are regular visitors. To the right of the hide, there is an artificial Sand Martin bank that was constructed to encourage these summer visitors to nest. It has been quite successful, though bird numbers vary from year to year. They made a welcome return in 2008. In winter this area is used as a feeding station, which attracts a variety of species, including Chaffinch, Greenfinch, Bullfinch, tit species, thrushes, Reed Buntings and Jay. Brambling are occasional visitors in winter. In September 2008, two Hawfinches were seen in this area. Water Rail frequent the pool edges, often being very vocal. The second hide overlooks a marshy pool that attracts Grey Heron and Snipe in winter. Reed Warblers have started to breed here. Foxes are regularly seen from the hides.

Visitors often place bird food on the fence posts throughout the reserve. This has been going on for many years and consequently some of the birds can be remarkably tame, especially Robins, Dunnocks, Nuthatches, Great, Blue and Coal Tits. The gate alongside the canal is one of the favourite feeding areas. Photographers can get some good pictures here.

The Glamorgan Canal stretches both north and south. The track north is perhaps the more interesting, a flooded wood (Alder Carr) lies to the left and the canal is to the right. In winter look for roaming flocks of Siskin and Redpoll feeding in the Alders. In winter, species such as Fieldfare and Redwing and the resident thrushes are often seen in the meadows adjacent to the allotments. The canal-side trees are perfect for woodpeckers and the open water usually has Mallard, Moorhen and Little Grebe, as well as the secretive Water Rail. The 'lock' near the track is another favourite feeding station and Kingfishers are frequently seen there. Early morning is best for this species as joggers and dog walkers frighten them off later in the day. Beyond here, on the left, used to be a good spot to see Marsh Tit. They are now quite uncommon but they do still make the occasional appearance. Otters also use this area.

The River Taff runs along the edge of the site and can be accessed from Longwood Drive, adjacent to Radyr weir, some 300 metres before the final roundabout. Bird interest is limited here; however Kingfishers, Dippers and Goosanders might be encountered. In late autumn the Taff Trail attracts quite a lot of visitors, hoping to see the upstream migration of Atlantic Salmon and Sea Trout.

There is a guided bird walk around the Reserve on the third Saturday in each month, led by one of the wardens. Meet at Forest Farm at 10 a.m.

23 – TONGWYNLAIS
Castell Coch (ST 1382), Fforest Fawr (ST 1383) and Fforest Ganol
(ST 1483)

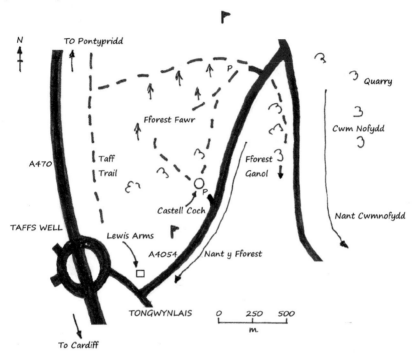

Access
Castell Coch is a well known landmark, situated above the Taff
Gorge. It lies to the north of Tongwynlais, adjacent to A470/Coryton
roundabout at Junction 32 of the M4. Take the A4054 into
Tongwynlais. Turn up Castle Road, alongside the Lewis Arms. The
Castle is about ½ kilometre up this road. The entrance is on the left,
just beyond the golf course. There is plenty of parking space.
Wheelchair users could access this area but might struggle elsewhere.

Fforest Fawr and Fforest Ganol lie a further kilometre up the
lane. Forest Fawr lies to the north of the road, whilst Fforest Ganol
and Cwm Nofydd are to the south. There is a car park in Fforest
Fawr. It is best to park near the entrance, as the main car park has
acquired an unsavoury reputation in recent times. There is an
information board with a map at the entrance to Fforest Ganol.

When to visit

Winter and spring are probably best, before the leaves develop.

These sites can be visited separately or there are a series of way-marked footpaths and bridleways that link them. A woodland path runs from Castell Coch to Fforest Fawr. The circular walk takes about an hour. Some of the paths are quite steep and can become quite muddy. These sites have many mature Beech and Hornbeam trees, both of which are relatively uncommon in Glamorgan.

Around the car parks are the regular woodland species. Chaffinches tend to dominate, although in the winter, Bramblings are sometimes attracted to the Beech mast. The winter of 2007/8 saw an unprecedented influx of this species. A flock of 500-1000 birds was seen roaming through these woods. All three woodpeckers can be found here, although, as ever the Lesser Spotted is very elusive. The Fforest Fawr site has a greater variety of habitats than Castell Coch. It backs on to the Castell Heights Golf Course, meaning woodland-edge lovers such as Mistle Thrush and Green Woodpecker are more likely to occur. The Brambling flock, mentioned above, favoured the car-park area. Species such as Goldcrest, Siskin, Treecreeper and Nuthatch are all relatively common.

It is worth exploring the woodland (Fforest Ganol/Cwm Nofydd) on the southern side of the road, alongside the information board. Follow the path up in to the woods. Walking boots or wellingtons are recommended, as the path gets churned up by horse riders and mountain bikers. A sought after species that might be found here is the Hawfinch. They are attracted to the Hornbeam. They are notoriously difficult to see as they are very shy and spend much of their time in the canopy. You might be lucky however. Some years ago a group of 20 were seen at nearby Tair-onnen. Check the ivy-covered trees above the path. This area also has Marsh Tit. A seasonal stream runs down the side of the road, attracting Grey Wagtails and Grey Heron.

A September visit might produce some passage migrants. In recent years both Spotted and Pied Flycatchers have passed through. Indeed Pied Flycatcher bred in this area in 2008.

* Footnote: Parc Cefn Onn is covered in the Caerphilly section

Area 4 : MERTHYR TYDFIL

Site 24 South Merthyr Tydfil
Site 25 Llwyn-on Reservoir
Site 26 Cadair Fawr
Site 27 Garwnant Forest Centre

Raven – Bob Mitchell

24 – SOUTH MERTHYR TYDFIL
Gethin Woods (SO 0403) and Blaencanaid (SO 0304)

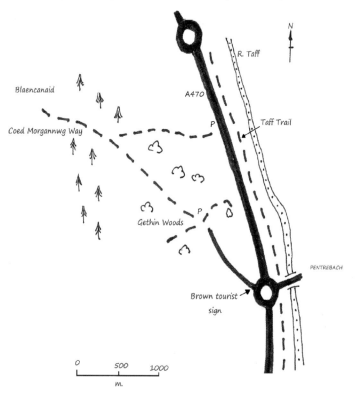

Access

These sites lie on the boundary of the Brecon Beacons National Park. Gethin Woods are located just to the south of Merthyr Tydfil. Take the A470 north towards Merthyr Tydfil. At the Pentrebach roundabout there is a brown tourist sign on the left, indicating the woods. Turn off here and there is a car park some 200 – 300 metres on the right. Beware as the top of the access road is a little rough. There are good views over the Taff valley from the car park. Paths lead off in several directions from the car park. Unfortunately none of them are accessible for wheelchair users. The Taff Trail passes to the east of the site.

When to visit

Probably best in spring/summer. There are BBQ facilities in the car park area. As a result it can get quite busy at weekends. An early morning visit is therefore advised.

Gethin Woods are owned and managed by the Forestry Commission. There is a good mix of deciduous and coniferous trees. Around the car park there are open stands of Oak, which in summer are particularly attractive for Redstarts, Spotted Flycatchers, Willow Warblers and Chiffchaffs. Blackcaps and Garden Warblers are likely to be found in the lusher vegetation to the south of the car park. There are a number of holes in the trees, indicating the presence of breeding woodpeckers. Other typical woodland species, such as thrushes, tits, finches and owls are all to be found in the woods. Scanning the ridges can be productive, often giving good views of raptors such as Buzzard, Sparrowhawk and occasionally Goshawk. Ravens are regular in the area. (See note on Blaencanaid below) The conifers might hold Siskin, Redpoll and occasionally Crossbill. The clear fell areas look ideal for Nightjar, indeed one was heard churring in the summer of 2007. Below the car park, the area around Webbers Pond is set aside as a nature reserve.

Blaencanaid lies just to the north of Gethin Woods. It is particularly known for its Raven roost. An evening visit in late summer may be rewarded by the sight of over 200 birds gathering at dusk (numbers are lower in winter). It is best to get in position about an hour before dusk, the sight and the noise can be quite spectacular.

The whole of this area is probably under-watched. There are other potential sites that might be worth checking whilst in the area: Firstly there is the Dan-y-Darren quarry (SO 0210). At the Merthyr roundabout there is a green sign on the left 'Coed Taf Fawr', where there is a small parking space. From here there is the opportunity to view the scree and the quarry on the opposite (eastern) side of the valley. A telescope is recommended.

Secondly, there is the Taf Fechan WTSWW Reserve (S0 0308). This ancient broad-leaved woodland reserve contains some spectacular limestone scenery. As well as the Taf Fechan Gorge, there is a small area of limestone pavement. The reserve follows the gorge south from the Blue Pool to Cefn Coed-y-Cymmer. Access can be gained in three places; at the Cefn Coed bridge (S0 037076), in the middle by way of a footpath, north of Trefechan and at the Blue Pool (SO 045097). These paths can become quite slippery. This reserve is not suitable for wheelchair users.

25 - LLWYN-ON RESERVOIR (SO 0111)

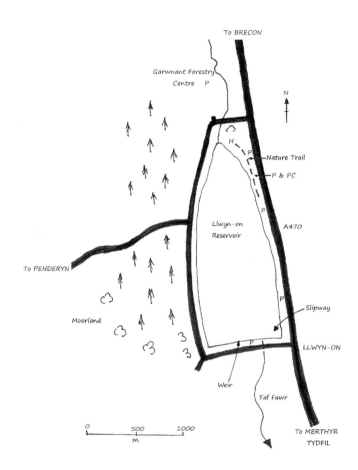

Access

Llwyn-on Reservoir lies some 3-4 kilometres north of Merthyr Tydfil. From Merthyr Tydfil, take the A470 towards Brecon. After passing through the village of Llwyn-on, look for a B & B sign on the left hand side. There are several access points, however only two are described:

1. The dam wall - a left turn, signposted to Cwm Cadlan, crosses the dam on a narrow road. It is best to park near the tower, as far off road as possible or alternatively park at the far end and walk back across the dam wall.

2. Reservoir car parks - there are three lay-bys on the road side which can get very busy in summer. There is a small toilet in the middle car park. Welsh Water has provided a bird watching hide at the northern end of the reservoir.

Wheelchair users should be able to scan from the lay-bys.

When to visit
Spring/summer is best, although there are birds around in winter.

Lying on the edge of the Brecon Beacons National Park, Llwyn-on is the southernmost of the three reservoirs in the Taff Fawr valley. (The other two are the Cantref and Beacons Reservoirs).

The site is very popular with fishermen, however disturbance is generally minimal. The water is quite deep and as a result it isn't particularly attractive for waders and wildfowl. However when water levels are low some mud is exposed, attracting waders. A telescope is recommended for scanning the lake surface and banks.

In winter, Tufted Duck, Teal, Mallard and Goldeneye might be seen but they are never very numerous. Coot, Cormorant, Great Crested Grebe, Little Grebe, Black-headed and Lesser Black-backed Gulls can be found on the water. It is worth checking the reservoir sides for Pied and Grey Wagtails and Grey Heron. The overflow spillway in the south-east corner of the reservoir has held Water Pipit in the past few winters and the local streams have Dipper and Kingfisher.

Common Sandpiper and Osprey are regular passage migrants. Wood Warblers regularly stop off on passage but don't appear to breed in the area. This part of northern Glamorgan is one of the few sites where Red Kite can reasonably be expected. Buzzards are quite common and Goshawk might be encountered.

At the northern end of the reservoir, Welsh Water has created a nature trail with a bird watching hide. At the time of writing, access was restricted as the hide was under repair. It is intended to re-open it in the near future. Park in the small car park at the extreme end of the reservoir and drop down on to the nature trail path that follows the reservoir edge, eventually reaching a belt of trees. Typical woodland species are to be found here. The hide is tucked away in the trees and overlooks a small reedy area and a shallow lagoon. This allows views of the local heronry. Kingfishers are fairly regular here also. It must be said however that the hide does not afford any great advantage and most species can be seen from other vantage points.

Red Kite – Paul Parsons

Another area that is recommended for birding is on the western side of the reservoir. Cross over the dam and park discretely. From here good views of the whole of the reservoir can be obtained. If parking is problematical, alternative access is possible from the Garwnant Forestry Centre, at the northern end of the reservoir.

A belt of pines runs alongside the edge of the western edge of the reservoir and this is attractive for species such as Siskin, Redpoll, and Coal Tit etc. Both Crossbill and Brambling have been recorded here in winter. This is one of the few areas where Willow Tits can be found in Glamorgan. Welsh Water has rangers on site. To date they have amassed a bird list of 120 species.

The Taff valley north of Merthyr Tydfil

The A470 Merthyr-Brecon road with Darren Fach on the right

The hillsides above Llwyn-on reservoir are perfect for raptors

The uplands

The head of the Rhondda Fawr overlooking Blaenrhondda

The flat topped moor lands of Cwm Cadlan

26 – CADAIR FAWR
Cefn Sychbant (SN 9810) and Cwm Cadlan (SN 9609)

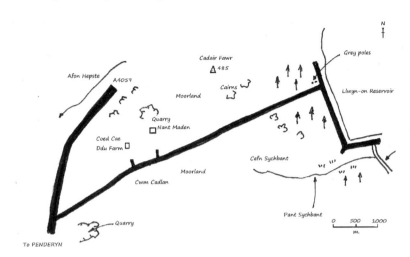

Access

After checking Llwyn-on reservoir, it is well worth heading for the moors of Cefn Sychbant and Cwm Cadlan. These sites actually lie within the Rhondda Cynon Taff authority boundary but are more easily accessed from Merthyr. After crossing the Llwyn-on dam, turn right and follow the narrow lane that runs alongside the western edge of the reservoir. There is a left turn about half way along this lane. This turn is easy to miss. Look for two upright grey poles next to the left turn. Follow this lane through the forestry. If approaching from the north, i.e. from the Garwnant Forestry Centre, take the turning signposted 'Cwm Cadlan.

The forestry land formerly had car parks but unfortunately they have all been closed recently. After about 1 kilometre, there is a cattle grid. From here the landscape changes dramatically from woodland to open moorland with numerous rocky outcrops. The road is very narrow and there are limited opportunities for parking.

When to visit

Summer is best but passage times and winter can prove interesting.

Lying over 400 metres above sea level, this site has some relatively rare habitats in Glamorgan. The moors can appear quite bleak, however there are birds here that cannot be easily found elsewhere in the county. Once up on the moorland, pull over regularly to scan the area. In summer, check the rocky cairns that are scattered throughout as Wheatears can often be seen on top of them. There are scattered farm buildings that are attractive for some bird species. For example, around Nant-maden farm (SO 963105), the dry stone walls are a good place to see both Wheatear and Stonechat. The farm buildings are attractive for Swallows and House Martins.

On the moors waders such as Curlew, Snipe and Golden Plover may be present. In the boggy areas of Cefn Sychbant, Grasshopper Warbler and Reed Bunting can be found. Also in summer Red Kite and Buzzard may be present. Other birds that you are certain to observe here are Skylark and Meadow Pipit. An autumn visit might produce passage birds. Ring Ouzels tend to favour the Rowans that border the moor. Up to 12 were present in autumn 2007.

The area can be very quiet in winter but perseverance can bring rewards. Merlin and Hen Harrier are possible in this season. Fieldfare and Redwing are two other species that can be found feeding on the Rowan berries. There is also normally a sizeable Starling flock roaming over this area in the winter. Corvid species such as Carrion Crow, Raven and Jackdaw are ever present.

Golden Plover – Colin Richards

27 - GARWNANT (SO 0013)

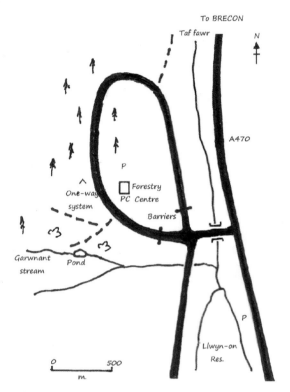

Access

Situated in the Coed Taf Fawr, the Forestry Commission has built a Visitor Centre at Garwnant. It lies just to the north of the Llwyn-on reservoir and is well signposted from the main A470 road. (Look for the 'Grey Heron' signs). A sharp left turn leads on to a bridge over the Taf Fawr. It is well worth stopping off here in order to scan the river for Dippers..

The road then winds up the slope to the right, under the barrier, towards the car park, via a one-way system. There are café and toilet facilities here and a childrens' play area. Wheelchair users should be able to access much of this site.

[Note that the car park barriers are closed at 6 p.m.]

When to visit

Spring/Summer is probably best.

The Forestry Centre attracts a lot of visitors, especially on summer weekends. For peace and quiet, head away from the car park/play area.

There are two way-marked trails – the Wern walk which is 2-3 kilometres in length and the shorter Willow walk. The former sets off from the Centre, past the ruins of Wern Farm and rises steeply on to the forest road. There are some good views from here. You are likely to encounter Goldcrest, which should be easily located in the conifers. This is also an excellent area to seek out Redpoll, Siskin and Crossbill. The Willow walk follows the Garwnant stream, where there are rapids and ponds that are worth checking. The ponds can be good for dragonflies in the summer. Most of the site has coniferous trees but there are deciduous trees lining the stream sides. Leaf warblers can be found here along with wagtails and Kingfishers. Grey Herons, probably from the Llwyn-on heronry, are often seen in the stream. The trees can hold Redstart and Tree Pipit. The best place to see Dipper is at the Taf Fawr bridge, mentioned in the access section.

* At the time of writing the café and toilets were closed for re-furbishment. For information, call the Forestry Commission on 08456 040845.

Area 5 : NEATH-PORT TALBOT

Site 28 Eglwys Nunydd Reservoir
Site 29 Margam Country Park
Site 30 Afan Forest Park
Site 31 Resolven
Site 32 Pontneddfechan

Wheatear – Bob Mitchell

28 - EGLWYS NUNYDD RESERVOIR (SS 7984)

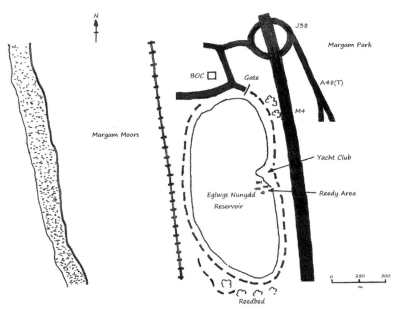

Access

Eglwys Nunydd is the largest fresh water body in Glamorgan, (100 hectares). Leaving the M4 at Junction 38, take the roundabout and go past the BOC works. Entry is via a metal gate on the left. This is a private site, owned by Corus. Some of the site was formerly part of a Glamorgan Wildlife Trust Reserve. Bona-fide birdwatchers haven't had any problems gaining access in the past. Wardens patrol the site and birders should be prepared to explain the reason for their visit. A road follows the perimeter of the reservoir. It is primarily used by anglers, dog walkers and yachtsmen. Vehicular access, when open, is only as far as the south-east corner. Wheelchair users may scan the reservoir from the road but be mindful of traffic entering the Yacht Club. There are no public facilities.

When to visit

Winter is undoubtedly the best season, although passage times can be interesting. Early morning viewing is best at the weekend. Yachts tend to disturb the birds later on.

Divers, duck and grebes are undoubtedly the main attractions at this site. Scanning the lake can be difficult in windy conditons, as quite sizeable waves can be generated. Large gatherings of Pochard, Tufted Duck and Goldeneye are regular in winter. Sometimes the flocks of duck commute between here and Kenfig Pool.

The ducks generally tend to gather in the bays around the Yacht Club, although the southern end of the reservoir is also worthy of investigation. Great Crested Grebe numbers tend to build up as winter progresses. On one particularly cold winters day in November 1988, five different grebe species were present - Great Crested, Little, Red-necked, Slavonian and Black-necked. Sawbills are regular with both Goosander and Smew having been recorded. The site has attracted many rarities. Perhaps the rarest ducks were Surf Scoters, which been recorded twice, in 1981 and 2003. Common and Velvet Scoters are more likely however and Long-tailed Ducks are now quite regular. Several gull species are attracted to the site. The highlight was undoubtedly the Franklin's Gull in October – November 1998. Other rare gulls have included Glaucous and Iceland Gulls, although the former has out-numbered the latter in recent years. Little Gull is now almost annual. Don't discount the hedgerow cum scrub that runs along the road side. Winter thrushes are found here, as are Goldcrests and over wintering Chiffchaffs and Blackcaps.

Spring and autumn can produce passage birds. Terns often drop in, especially Common, Arctic and Black. The reservoir is also a magnet for hirundines and Swifts. The concrete banks are not ideal for waders but passage Common Sandpiper and Yellow Wagtail are almost annual. Other waders may visit briefly, notably Grey Phalaropes, after autumn gales. These weather conditions have also brought Leach's Petrels to the reservoir, particularly the 'wreck' of December 2005. A roosting flock of Lapwings is often present.

Summer is generally unproductive, however there are breeding Great Crested Grebe, Little Grebe, Mute Swan, Willow Warbler, Sedge Warbler, Reed Warbler, Whitethroat and Reed Bunting. Woodpeckers are also recorded and Kingfishers have been seen at the northern end. The reed bed at the southern end is worthy of exploration as are Margam Moors, where birds of prey may be found. Access the moors by continuing down the lane, past the BOC works.

29 - MARGAM COUNTRY PARK (SS 8086)

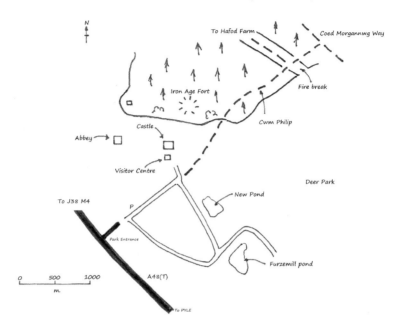

Access

Margam Park lies to the north-east of the A48, adjacent to Port Talbot steelworks. It is an area of parkland, approximately 350 hectares in size. It contains an 18th Century Orangery, a Tudor Gothic Victorian Mansion and an Iron Age Fort. There is plenty of parking available. Wheelchair users should be able to access most of the park. Note that there is an entrance fee. The Park's telephone number is 01639 881635.

When to visit

Spring is the best time to visit but it is pleasant at any time of year. Its popularity means that it very busy at weekends and bank holidays. For bird watching it is best to head away from the crowds and use one of the trails. These trails can be quite steep in places and are not suitable for wheelchair users.

On the ridge there is a large area of coniferous woodland. Elsewhere deciduous species such as Oak, Beech and Sweet Chestnut are found. There are four colour coded walks, for which a leaflet is available. The more adventurous may wish to access the

Coed Morgannwg Way and the Ogwr Ridgeway Walks that link up
with the park trails. A recommended walk is through Cwm Philip,
where the lower slopes have been replanted with Oak, Beech, Rowan,
Birch and Ash. Look for a variety of woodland species, such as
Treecreeper, Great Spotted and Green Woodpeckers, Jay, Goldcrest,
Nuthatch, Sparrowhawk and Siskin. In the summer this is a good
spot to seek out warblers such as Blackcap, Chiffchaff and Willow
Warbler. The boggy valley floor with its tussock grass is ideal
habitat in winter for Woodcock and Snipe.

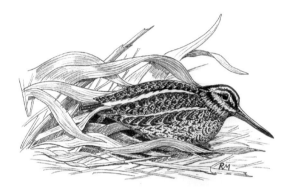

Snipe – Bob Mitchell

At the end of the valley there is a gate, from which the path
then passes up a steep track to the right and follows the boundary
wall of the park. This rises to approximately 250 metres. The
energetic can access the Hafod Farm area (See the north-west
Maesteg site guide) by trekking north-east across Mynydd Margam,
following the main fire break in the forest. It is always worth
checking out the forest clearings as Great Grey Shrikes have over-
wintered in the past.

Elsewhere the grassland on the approach to Furzemill Pond is
a favourite spot to see the Park's herd of grazing deer. The grassy
scrub areas around Furzemill and New Pond are worth checking out
for Reed Bunting and Stonechat. Whinchat has been recorded and
Skylarks can be seen on the open grassland. Take care walking
across this area as it is has hidden drainage ditches. These however
attract frogs and consequently Grey Herons. On the island in New
Pond, Coot, Mallard and Moorhen have nested, as has Mandarin
Duck. Winter visitors to the pond have included Pochard and
Gadwall.

30 - AFAN FOREST PARK (SS 8194)

No sketch map is provided for this site. The area is vast and there are numerous trails. Detailed maps are available in the Visitor Centre.

Access

Situated in the Afan Valley, just to the north of Pontrhydyfen, this park covers some 6000 hectares. It has acquired the nickname of 'Little Switzerland' because of its thickly forested hills. From Junction 40 of the M4, take the A4107 north for about 10 kilometres. Look for the brown tourist signs for the Afan Park Visitor Centre. There are toilets and a café available at the Visitor Centre. The South Wales Miners' Museum is also situated here. Neath-Port Talbot authority is developing this area for activities such as mountain biking, rambling etc There are nine colour coded way trails, parts of which are accessible for wheelchairs. Call 01639 686868 for information.

When to visit

Any time of year can be productive although if you want a chance of seeing the Honey Buzzards, late May/early June is recommended.

Situated amongst some stunning scenery, the forests of the Afan Valley have attracted a lot of interest in recent years, mainly because Honey Buzzards have been discovered in the area. Normally bird watching guides shy away from advertising the location of scarce breeding birds. In this case however their presence has been widely publicised by the likes of the Welsh Raptor Research Group, Neath Port-Talbot Council and the Forestry Commission. Indeed there are cameras sending web-cam images of these birds back to the Visitor Centre.

Honey Buzzards are very secretive and are notoriously difficult to see. Take care as there are plenty of Common Buzzards in the area. As stated above, the best chance of seeing Honey Buzzards is in late May/early June, soon after they arrive in the country and begin their soaring courtship displays. Plenty of patience will be needed to catch a glimpse of these scarce birds. Position yourself in a spot with a good view over the forest canopy and keep your eyes peeled. The cuckoo-like head and flat wings are the main diagnostic features. They have been intensively studied and it has been found that apart from the traditional diet of wasps, a major part of the Afan Forest birds' diet is made up of frogs.

Honey Buzzard – Bob Mitchell

Apart from the very rare Honey Buzzard, the park holds a good variety of bird species. The park has a variety of habitats and these naturally dictate the range of species that may be encountered. Common woodland birds such as Great Spotted and Green Woodpeckers, Nuthatch, Treecreeper, Wren, Bullfinch, Jay, thrushes, tits and finches are likely to be seen.

Many of the commoner species are attracted to the feeders outside the Visitor Centre. The fast flowing streams attract Dipper, Grey Heron and Kingfisher, whilst the damp wooded areas may have Woodcock. In summer the deciduous woods are likely to have migrants such as Redstart, Tree Pipit, Willow and Garden Warblers, Pied and Spotted Flycatcher as well as Chiffchaff. The conifers hold Goldcrests, Coal Tits, Siskin and Crossbill. Whilst scanning for Honey Buzzards, other birds of prey are likely to be seen over the forests. Apart from Buzzard and Sparrowhawk, Goshawk and Red Kite are occasionally seen in the park.

31 - RESOLVEN (SN 8202)

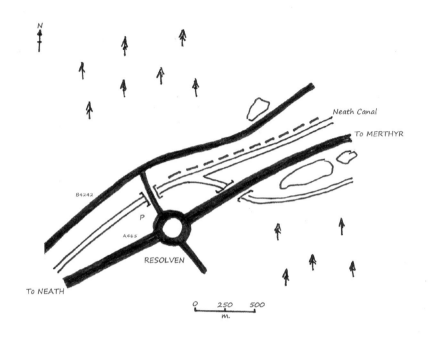

Access

Resolven lies on the main A465 Merthyr-Neath road. At the Resolven roundabout, turn off towards the village. There are brown tourist signs for the Neath Canal. Almost immediately there is a car park on your left, (The Resolven Canal Car Park) where toilets are available. Wheelchair users should not be disadvantaged at this site.

When to visit

For displaying Goshawks visit in March or April, for Honey Buzzards, visit in late May/early June.

The car park provides an excellent vantage point to scan for raptors. Apart from Honey Buzzards, there are Goshawk, Buzzard, Red Kite, Peregrine, Merlin, Sparrowhawk and Kestrel in the area. The RSPB have set up telescopes to help spot these birds. If you fancy a walk there is a footpath alongside the Canal, from where birds of prey can be also seen, plus a good variety of passerines.

From Resolven it is worth checking the lakes alongside the A465. Lying about 3 kilometres north-east of Resolven, there are two lakes (one of which is used for water sports). They are only viewable from the south bound carriageway and access is limited. You will need to park in the lay-by and walk back towards the lakes. They don't usually attract large numbers of birds but Great Crested Grebe and Goosander are fairly regular in winter.

Another site one might consider visiting is the Aberdulais Falls (SS 7799) on the River Neath. Park alongside the British Legion in Station Road. There is also access on the other side of the river. The fast flowing water and rocky bed of the river provide ideal conditions for Dipper, Grey and Pied Wagtail, Grey Heron and on passage, Common Sandpiper. Another waterfall site nearby is the Melincourt Falls WTSWW Reserve (SN 825017), where similar species are likely to be found. Don't forget to look up, as many raptors follow the river valleys as they migrate.

Cormorant - Paul Parsons

32 - PONTNEDDFECHAN (SN 9007)

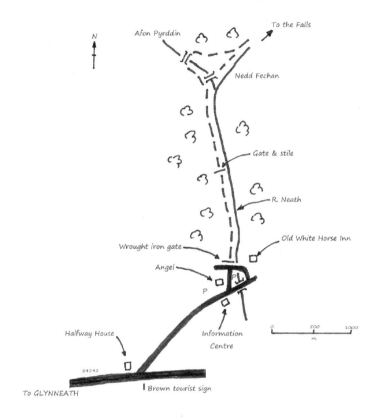

Access

Lying on the Glamorgan–Powys boundary, the Pontneddfechan area is right on the edge of the Brecon Beacons National Park. From Glyn-neath, take the A4242 and follow the signs for Pontneddfechan. (Some of the older signs use the anglicised version of Pontneathvaughan). After passing the Dinas Rock Hotel, carry on along this road for a couple of kilometres, keeping an eye out for the Halfway House on the left. A brown tourist sign directs you to Pontneddfechan. The Waterfall Information Centre is on your right and the Angel pub is on the left. There is a large car park opposite the Information Centre and a smaller one behind the pub. Look for some wrought iron gates, which have the words 'SGWD GWLADYS' on them. There is a

91

Riverside species

As the rivers have become cleaner, Kingfishers can now be found along major rivers

Following the decline of the coal industry, Dippers have re-colonised many rivers

Reed bed specialists

Bearded Tits are now regular winter visitors and are a potential breeding species

Winter also brings Bitterns to reed beds in the country

very good map of the area on the information board. It states that the walk should take about 45 minutes – it will probably take longer, especially if you stop to scan for birds or to take in the spectacular scenery. Initially the path is reasonably level. It can become quite muddy after rain and walking boots are recommended. It is not suitable for wheelchair users. After the river confluence the path is a lot steeper and may be quite slippery.

Before your walk, it is recommended that you visit the Information Centre. There are displays and numerous maps are available. There is also plenty of information about the geology and archaeological features of the area. Call 01639 721795.

When to visit
Spring/early summer

This scenic riverside walk is one of the prettiest in the county. Even if the birds are thin on the ground, the scenery is impressive and the falls are certainly worth a visit. The area is excellent for seeing some of the Welsh upland specialities. The fast flowing River Neath is an excellent spot for seeing Dipper and with luck Kingfisher, Goosander and Grey Wagtail.

Pied Flycatcher – Bob Mitchell

The riverside slopes are dominated by Sessile Oaks, with a mix of Hazel, Birch and Rowan. In spring, Redstart, Wood Warbler, Pied and Spotted Flycatcher should be seen. If you don't fancy walking all the way to the falls, most of the 'special' birds of the area should make an appearance before reaching the confluence of the Nedd Fechan and Afon Pyrddin. With the contraction of the range of these species, this is now one of the best areas in the county to see them. Also in the woods are many of our commoner woodland species, in particular look out for Redpoll and Siskin. The dense tree canopy means that overhead observation is difficult. Raven are fairly evident, as are Buzzards. Other raptor species that might be glimpsed are Red Kite, Goshawk and Sparrowhawk.

Similar species are likely to be encountered in Blaenant-y-Gwyddyl WTSWW Reserve (SN 885076). Turn off the A465 at Glyn-neath and follow the A4109 north. Park at Lon-y-nant and cross the stile at the top of the road. This site is not suitable for wheelchair users.

Area 6 : RHONDDA CYNON TAFF

Site 33 Llanwonno
Site 34 Parc Cwm Dare
Site 35 Tirfounder Fields
Site 36 Pwll Gwaun Cynon
Site 37 Barry Sidings
Site 38 Glyncornel Woods

Peregrine Falcon – Colin Richards

33 - LLANWONNO (ST 0395)

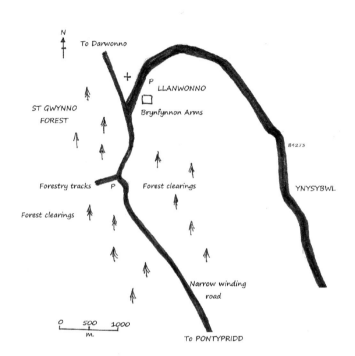

Access

Llanwonno is a small settlement in the heart of the St. Gwynno Forest, just to the north of Pontypridd. From Gelliwasted Road in central Pontypridd turn up Gelliwasted Grove and cross the railway line alongside Pontypridd Library. The road meanders up towards Graigwen. Eventually at the top of the hill there is a cattle grid after which there is open countryside. Follow this narrow country road for approximately 5 kilometres, as far as the Brynfynnon Arms pub. There is some parking below the pub. Alternatively the site may be reached from Ynysybwl by following the B4273 road through Ynysybwl, past Mynachdy. Look for the signs for Llanwonno. Take a left turn towards the forestry and the Brynfynnon Arms. The only facilities are in the pub. From here the area can be explored on foot. To access the best Nightjar sites walk along the lane towards Pontypridd, a distance of approximately 1 kilometre. There is limited parking on the road side, which can reduce the amount of walking. Wheelchair users can access many areas, although some of the forestry tracks are a little rough. Try not to leave cars unattended for long periods.

When to visit

The last week of May/early June are best for Nightjars, whilst January/February are best for Woodcock.

This is a large area of forestry surrounding the hamlet of Llanwonno. The pub is quite central and is probably the best starting point for exploration. The area is best known for its Nightjars but holds many other species too. Nightjars prefer relatively young conifers or recent clear-fell, over which they can 'hawk' for moths etc. The best sites in recent years have been at ST 033948/ST 032942 (limited parking). These sites are slightly elevated and give reasonable all round views. As the conifers grow the birds tend to move to fresh areas that are more to their liking. There are several other suitable areas of forestry where Nightjars might be seen. A dusk visit, on a calm night in early summer should produce 'churring' birds. Don't forget the insect repellent! Other birds that might be seen are Goshawk, Redpoll, Linnet, Meadow Pipit, Tree Pipit, Tawny Owl, Cuckoo and Grasshopper Warbler.

A winter visit might produce Woodcock. In recent winters they have been seen from the Bryfynnon Arms car park at dawn or dusk. This area has supported an over-wintering Great Grey Shrike on a couple of occasions. It is difficult to give a guide as to the whereabouts of this species, as they are quite mobile. Look carefully in the clear fell areas, where they could set up a winter territory.

Nightjars – Bob Mitchell

34 - PARC CWM DARE (SN 9802)

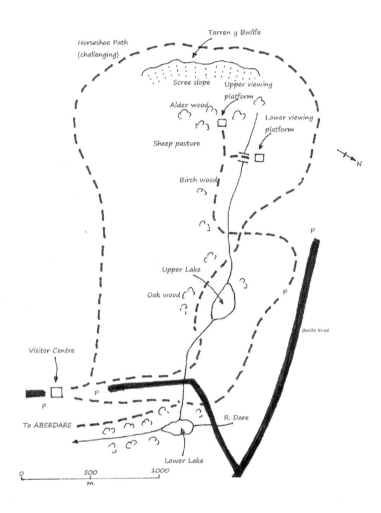

Access

Take the A4059 to Aberdare. Follow the one-way system in Aberdare town centre, bearing left at the war memorial. At the statue, head up Monk Street. Half way up the hill, on the right, is a brown tourist sign indicating the park. Turn right in to Highland Place. The entrance to the park is on your left, just beyond St. Margaret's School. From here a long driveway leads up towards the Visitor Centre where there is ample space for car parking. There are a number of walks, varying in difficulty, some of which are accessible for wheelchair users. The Visitor Centre can provide maps of the park and there are information boards dotted throughout. There are a café and toilets in the centre, which is open from 9 a.m. – 7 p.m. Call 01685 874672. At the time of writing the Visitor Centre was being refurbished.

When to visit

Can be productive at any time of year. For the Peregrines however, a late spring/early summer visit is recommended.

It is worth checking the feeders at the rear of the Visitor Centre. A good variety of species are attracted to them. Siskin and Coal Tit are regular. In winter, both Willow and Marsh Tits have been seen. It might be worth popping in to the café in summer as there is a live TV feed giving views of the Peregrines that nest in the park. Unfortunately the cameras were vandalised in the summer of 2008. It is to be hoped that they are up and running again soon.

There are a number of walks ranging from the long-distance Coed Morgannwg Way, leading all the way to Margam Park, down to a relatively easy stroll on the Bwllfa Trail. To see a good variety of species, take the Bwllfa Trail from the Visitor Centre towards the Upper Lake. The path skirts a small stream where Kingfishers, Dippers and Grey Wagtails can be seen. A springtime visit should allow you to hear warblers such as Blackcap and Chiffchaff. Typical woodland species such as Long-tailed Tit, Bullfinch, Chaffinch and Greenfinch are likely. In winter, thrushes tend to gather to feed on the abundant berry bearing bushes. At the lake, the vista really opens up. Coot, Moorhen and Little Grebe are present all year round. The number of species builds up as winter approaches. Look for duck such as Tufted Duck, Pochard and Teal. Snipe can skulk around the reedy edges and Grey Heron are usually present. On passage, Common Sandpipers have been recorded. In the fields alongside, Grasshopper Warblers have been heard reeling in recent years and Reed Bunting can also be found.

From the lake, passing the site of the former Nant Melyn Colliery, Meadow Pipits can be seen on the impoverished grassland slopes. Here, an abandoned brick colliery building has been adapted to allow bats to roost. Higher up, Alder trees tend to dominate and this is an excellent spot to see Redpoll and Siskin. In spring, the rattling song of the Redstart appears to be everywhere. Spotted

Flycatchers are regular but it appears that Pied Flycatchers no longer breed here. Lesser Spotted Woodpecker has been recorded but they are typically difficult to find. It is thought that they are merely passing through and no longer breed in the park. Green and Great Spotted Woodpeckers should be more obliging. To access the viewing platforms, leave the Bwllfa Trail and set off up the hill.

The RSPB formerly ran a Peregrine Watch in the park. The viewing platforms are still in place, allowing visitors to see the Peregrines that nest on the Tarren y Bwllfa crags. The second platform is slightly higher up the hillside. Cross over the stile into the damp woodland alongside the lower viewing platform. The path can be a little slippery but the walk is worthwhile, as there are broad vistas of the crags and scree. With luck, the Peregrines should be on view. Merlins are also found in this area.

Ring Ouzel – Colin Richards

The logo of the park is the Ring Ouzel. These charismatic birds no longer breed in the park, however they are still breeding a few kilometres north in Powys. Nowadays the only real chance of seeing them in the park is in the autumn, as they pass through. Check the Rowan trees at the base of the crags. Alternatively take the Darren Horseshoe path (Craig Pen-rhiw-llech Trail) around the top of the crags and search the old tips to the east. Wheatear and Whinchat might also be encountered there. The latter is steadily moving north to breed, just like Ring Ouzel, Wood Warbler and Pied Flycatcher.

Returning to the Visitor Centre, consider taking the path to the Lower Lake, which passes through some nice deciduous woodland. Once again leaf warblers and woodpeckers are likely.

35 - TIRFOUNDER FIELDS (SO 0101)

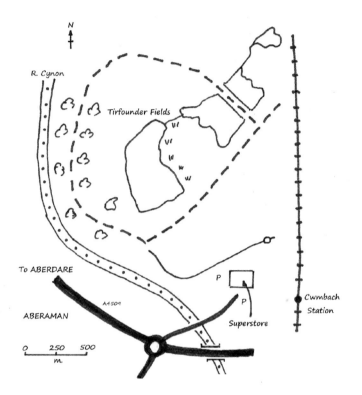

Access

Situated just south of Aberdare, this site lies on the flood plain of the River Cynon. Take the A4059 to Aberdare and look for the Superstore signs as you cross the Cynon at Cwmbach. From the roundabout, pass the Tirfounder Fields pub and the ASDA superstore. There should be somewhere to park on one of the service roads. The site is well served by public transport. Unfortunately there has been quite a lot of fly-tipping, making it look very untidy. A further problem has been the spread of Japanese Knotweed and Himalayan Balsam across the site. The local council are actively tackling these pernicious weeds. Don't be put off, this area has good bird watching potential. The footpaths have been improved as part of the Cynon Valley River Park scheme and there are tarmac tracks around the site. Wheelchairs users might be able to access some areas. Wellingtons are recommended as parts of the site can be wet.

When to visit

Probably best in winter.

The main target species is undoubtedly the Willow Tit. This is one of the few sites in the county where this species can be reliably encountered. They like the damp woodland areas of this site. Their buzzing calls can be heard in the riverside trees (not necessarily Willows) and Gorse. Other species that might be seen are Redpoll, Reed Bunting and Whitethroat.

From the path, one can glimpse the reedy ponds. These ponds attract species such as Grey Heron, Coot, Moorhen, Kingfisher, Dipper and Little Grebe. In summer, good numbers of hirundines and Swifts can be seen over the site. Unfortunately the Sand Martin colony appears to have been abandoned due to flooding of the nest holes. A late summer Hobby has been seen hunting over the site in the last couple of years. Both Reed and Sedge Warblers breed in the reed beds. Two relative newcomers to the site are Grasshopper and Cetti's Warblers. Two pairs of each were in the area in 2007.

Around the ponds Water Rails are present. Their squealing calls are very distinctive. On passage, species such as Green Sandpiper might be encountered. Occasionally they may over-winter. Also in winter, Teal are found on the ponds and both Snipe and Jack Snipe should be present. An evening visit might be rewarded with the sight of large numbers of Canada Geese coming in to roost. Recently a Barn Owl has been using the site. With extreme luck another recent arrival, the Otter may be seen. They have been gradually re-colonising the Cynon Valley.

Dipper – Alan Rosney

36 - PWLL GWAUN CYNON (ST 0399)

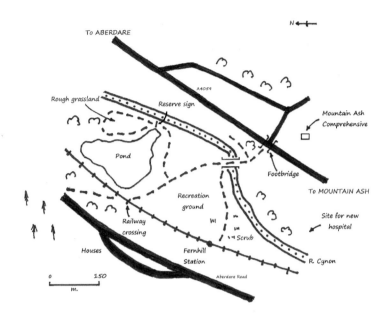

Access

This small WTSWW reserve (7.2 hectares) lies approximately 1 kilometre north of Mountain Ash. It is situated between the A4059 Aberdare to Mountain Ash road and the Aberaman to Mountain Ash road, south of the River Cynon. The site runs between the Cynon and the railway line. Access can be obtained from the public footpath crossing the reserve from the A4059, opposite Mountain Ash Comprehensive School, to the A4224. Parking is not easy, however there is a small pull-in. The reserve is immediately adjacent to Fernhill Railway Station and the Cynon Trail runs along the boundary. Unfortunately most of the site is not suitable for wheelchair use.

Time to visit

This evolving site may be visited throughout the year. It may not yet produce large numbers of birds but has the potential to do so.

Lord Aberdare donated this area to the Wildlife Trust in 1986. It is on the site of the infamous Phurnacite works. It had the reputation of being one of the most polluted sites in the U.K. Since the closure of the plant in the 1980's, the pond and surrounding areas have made a remarkable recovery and now support an impressive number of species. The pond has stands of Arrowheads, a scarce plant in Glamorgan. Other plants include Fat Duckweed, Water Chickweed, Marsh Yellow-cress, Great Pond Sedge and Common Club-rush. Unfortunately Japanese Knotweed and Himalayan Balsam are encroaching on to the site and Bulrushes appear to be spreading in the pond. The site appears good for invertebrates e.g. several dragonfly and damselfly species can be present.

The water bird species likely to be seen are breeding Little Grebe, Mallard, Moorhen and Coot. Reed Buntings can be found in the reedy areas. In autumn some gulls are present and hirundines visit to feed, prior to migration. As winter approaches a few duck species may visit the lake, with Tufted Duck and Pochard being the most likely. Teal, Gadwall and Goldeneye have all been recorded. A much rarer visitor was a Bittern, which over-wintered here in the past. Regular visitors include Kingfisher and Grey Heron. Both Otter and Mink are occasionally recorded here. On the nearby river, Dipper, wagtails and Common Sandpiper may be found.

There are a number of dead trees on the site that are obviously used by Great Spotted Woodpeckers. In the woods Redpoll, Siskin, Blackcap and Chaffinch can be found. Check the area around the station as Willow Tit has been seen there in the past. The surrounding hillsides are worth scanning for raptors.

Great Spotted Woodpecker – Alan Rosney

37 - BARRY SIDINGS (ST 0591)

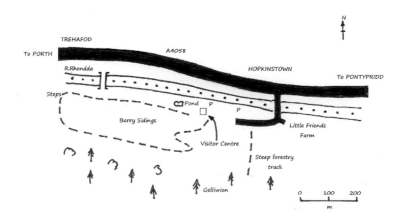

Access

The RCT Countryside Section developed this country park in the 1980's on the site of the former railway sidings. Being some 3.5 hectares in area, it follows the southern bank of the River Rhondda for about 1.5 kilometres.

Take the A4058 Rhondda road from Pontypridd. Once through Hopkinstown, look out for a narrow bridge across the river. (There is a sign showing "Little Friends Farm"). The site is easily accessed by public transport. A bus route passes along Gyfeillon Road and Trehafod railway station is only a short distance away.

At the entrance, the access road swings round to the right, leading to a large car park and onwards towards the Visitor Centre. A cafeteria and toilets are available in the Centre. Maps of the site can also be examined there. Most of the paths should be accessible for wheelchairs, although those branching off into the woods are definitely not.

When to visit

Any time of year should produce some birds.

Lying just below the Rhondda Heritage Park, this linear park follows the River Rhondda. There is a circular walk from the Centre which takes in several different habitats. A good variety of tits and finches should be encountered on the feeders around the Visitor Centre. There are a series of small fishing lakes where Mallard and Moorhen are to be found. In January 2009, a Little Egret visited these ponds.

The circular trail is some 1.7 kilometres in length. By taking the path towards Trehafod, there is a good view of the River Rhondda. Dippers are regular here and Goosanders can be seen in winter. Other riverside birds such as Grey Heron, Cormorant, Grey and Pied Wagtails are common. In summer, check the riverside vegetation for warblers such as Blackcap. The path northwards actually leaves the park and there is a short section that uses the road, so beware of traffic in this area. The trail then continues up a slope, past some houses. There are good views down the valley from this point. The trail continues at the end of the access road (between the two houses) and enters the Forestry Commission land of Gelliwion. This woodland consists mainly of Larch. Crossbills, Siskin, Redpoll and other finches and tits have been sighted. Buzzard and Raven are regular over the valley. A rarer visitor in the winter of 2007 was a Great Grey Shrike.

There is an alternative route into the Gelliwion forestry from the main car park. A steep path leads off into the woods.

Jackdaw – Paul Parsons

38 - GLYNCORNEL WOODS (SS 9994)

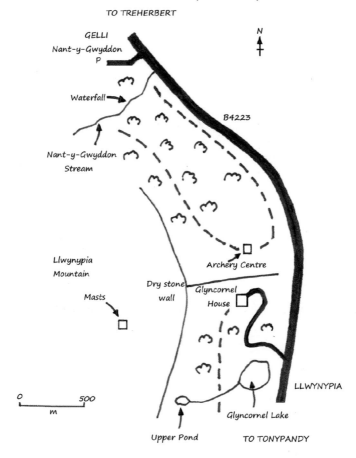

TO TREHERBERT

GELLI
Nant-y-Gwyddon
P

N

Waterfall

B4223

Nant-y-Gwyddon
Stream

Llwynypia
Mountain

Archery Centre

Dry stone
wall

Glyncornel

Masts

Glyncornel
House

0   500
m

LLWYNYPIA

Glyncornel Lake

Upper Pond   TO TONYPANDY

Access

Glyncornel LNR is in the Rhondda Fawr. It lies just off the B4223, to the north of Tonypandy, midway between Llwynypia and Gelli. There are several entrances to the reserve. Perhaps the best is the Forestry Commission Car Park at Nant-y-Gwyddon, (SS 987945) where there is enough parking space for about a dozen vehicles. There are no facilities on site. Being on a hillside with uneven trails, the site is unsuitable for wheelchair users. Boots are recommended, as the paths can be very wet.

When to visit

An early morning spring visit is probably best.

106

Glyncornel is an upland Oak wood, consisting mainly of sessile Oak. It forms part of the Craig Pont-Rhondda SSSI and has a rich array of ferns, and mosses. The bluebell display in spring is quite spectacular. It has the common woodland species such as woodpeckers, thrushes, finches and tits. Buzzards and Sparrowhawks may be overhead.

In spring, the woods are full of song, with the residents being joined by migrants such as Tree Pipit, Garden Warbler, Blackcap, Willow Warbler, Chiffchaff and Wood Warbler. Spotted Flycatchers breed in small numbers, though the once regular Pied Flycatcher has been scarce in recent years. Visitors may also like to look beyond the reserve itself and explore the adjacent hillside of Llwynypia Mountain. Skylark, Meadow Pipit, Stonechat and Reed Bunting are common, though numbers are low in winter. In summer Whinchat and Whitethroat breed and Cuckoo is often heard. Recently, after extensive felling of conifer plantations, Nightjars have been discovered churring. Generally however the summer months are quiet. In autumn and winter Fieldfare, Redwing and small flocks of Redpoll and Siskin often join the residents.

Redpoll – Paul Parsons

Several trails run through the woods. The first is from the Nant-y-Gwyddon car park. Go back to the car park entrance and turn right, following the wall for 15 metres, crossing the stream that descends the hillside. Grey Wagtail and occasionally Dipper may be there. Proceed through the kissing gate into the woods. Listen for the distinctive song of the Wood Warbler in late April or early May. After 30 metres there is a small open area to the right with several dead trees. Spotted Flycatchers often hunt insects here. Continue along the path until it leads to an open, grassed area where it divides. The right-hand path gradually ascends across the grassed area. In winter, look for finch flocks including Redpoll and Siskin. The path then leads to the Archery Centre, under the stone arch to the rear of Glyncornel House. Check the feeders on the front lawn. In the past, a pair of Spotted Flycatchers built their nest under the eaves. From the house, there are several options. Take any of the trails that return to the Nant-y-Gwyddon car park by going down the road from the house (or take the trail to the Upper Pond from the rear of the house). The road leads to Glyncornel Lake. Good views are afforded across the tall trees. Grey Heron, Mallard and Kingfisher may be seen and in winter, Goosander may be present.

A visit to the Upper Pond can be rewarding. Take the path from the rear of Glyncornel House, first checking the small stand of pines for Goldcrest and Coal Tit. Follow the wide trail away from the house, where the trees are very tall and there are fewer brambles. Green or Great Spotted Woodpeckers are often present. Continue on the path to the fence at the edge of the reserve. The small wooden bridge over the stream leads down to Station Terrace, alongside the lake. Alternatively, before crossing the bridge, take the poorly marked zig-zag trail leading up the steep hill. Cross the stream and follow the fence-line. The path eventually leads into a small quarry, the site of the Upper Pond. Kingfishers are often here in winter and dragonflies abound in summer. This is the highest point on the reserve and it marks the start of the return journey to the car park.

Follow the trail north for views of the canopy. When the house appears once more, take the right hand fork of the path. This follows a wall running down the hillside. Where the wall meets another, cross the stile and turn left into the small grass clearing surrounded by privet. The Archery Centre should be on the right. Proceed through the damp wooded area, passing over a small wooden path running alongside a small pool. Turn right as the trail splits and go into the open grassed area. After 20 metres, turn left into the woods once more. Keep on the main trail to the fence at the end of the reserve. This can be the most productive part of the reserve. It is bursting with song in early spring. Wood Warbler has been recorded here in the last few years. The trail finally leads through a wire fence and over the stream. This can be a good spot for Redstarts.

* **Footnote 1** : Llanilid (ST 9881) – The future of this site is uncertain. Had it been secure, Llanilid would certainly have featured in this guide. This old open cast site, adjacent to the M4, has a large lake, extensive short grassy areas and large areas of Gorse. All of these are scarce habitats in Glamorgan. Among breeding species are Dartford Warbler, Little Ringed Plover and Willow Tit. Species that regularly use the area for feeding and wintering are Barn and Short-eared Owls plus Hen Harriers. A Richard's Pipit over-wintered in 2003/4. Dormice have also been found on the site. The prospects are that it will be further developed for industry and housing.

* **Footnote 2** : Cadair Fawr is covered in the Merthyr section.

The Gower Peninsula

The scenic south Gower coast with Worm's Head in the background

Oxwich NNR is a superb area with a mix of habitat types

Recent colonists

Choughs have bred in Gower for many years and have now begun to breed on the Heritage Coast

Red Kites are advancing south from their stronghold in Mid Wales

Area 7 : SWANSEA & GOWER

Merlin – Bob Mitchell

39 – SWANSEA BAY
Blackpill (SS 6190) and Mumbles (SS 6387)

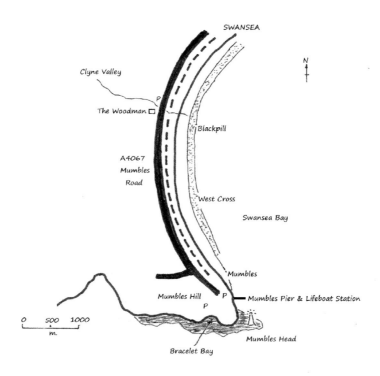

Access

The A4067 follows the shoreline of Swansea Bay west from the city of Swansea round to Mumbles Head. Access is possible along most of its length by crossing the disused line of the old Mumbles railway, which now forms the Swansea Bay cycle path.

Undoubtedly the two best sites to visit are Blackpill and Mumbles Pier. Car parking is relatively easy. There are pay and display car parks at both sites. At Blackpill, there is also some parking alongside the Woodman pub. (The Woodman car park is split into two parts – the area nearest the road is for pub customers. Birders should park on the far side). The whole area is also easily accessible via public transport. Facilities are plentiful throughout and both sites are accessible for wheelchairs.

When to visit

Winter and passage periods are best. Check the tide times. Ideally, visit a couple of hours before high tide. The mud flats at Blackpill are the last area of Swansea Bay to be covered by the tide. Waders and gulls can gather in large numbers.

The shoreline of Swansea Bay extends for over 17½ kilometres, the whole length being backed by the conurbation of Swansea and its suburbs. The tidal flats, especially in the west, extend up to 1½ kilometres from the shore.

The best known site is undoubtedly Blackpill (SS 619906). The closure of two nearby rubbish tips in recent years and the cleaning of the beach have meant reduced feeding opportunities for the gulls, hence a decline in their numbers. A telescope is vital at this site. When windy, the best place to stand is in the lee of the shelter. Getting the tide right is critical. By visiting before high tide, the birds are slowly pushed up the beach towards you. Get it wrong and they are likely to be a very long way off. It is recommended to be in place at least an hour either side of high water on Neap tides and two hours on Spring tides. A minor irritation for bird watchers can be the number of dog walkers and joggers that regularly scatter the flocks.

Blackpill first hit the birding headlines in 1973. On 14th March of that year, the first Ring-billed Gull for Britain and Ireland was found. They were subsequently recorded regularly. In recent years their numbers have declined somewhat. Careful watching still turns up the occasional bird, often in the West Cross area. Even without a Ring-bill present, Blackpill is certainly the place for gull watching, with all the familiar species present. Common Gulls may number hundreds, even in mid-summer, despite there being no large colonies nearby. Black-headed Gulls can be even more numerous. Mediterranean Gulls are now regular here. Up to 40 have been present, with colour-ringed birds from colonies in Belgium, Holland and Hungary being identified. The small car park (with the Big Apple) at Bracelet Bay (SS 630870) just beyond Mumbles Head is a good spot to catch up with Med. Gulls in varying plumages. Numbers are at their lowest in mid-winter. Little Gulls may be seen in virtually any month, either at Blackpill or further west at Mumbles. The list of gulls is impressive with Ivory, Ross's, Sabine's, Iceland, Kumlien's, Glaucous and Yellow-legged Gulls being recorded.

The mud flats at Blackpill are good for waders. Large numbers of Oystercatchers are present throughout the year. Ringed Plover, Dunlin, Bar-tailed Godwit, Curlew and Redshank occur throughout the year, though they may be scarce in summer. Dunlins are by far the most numerous. Other waders regularly seen include Grey Plover, Knot and Sanderling. Curlew Sandpiper, Black-tailed Godwit, Greenshank and Whimbrel come through on passage.

Whilst at Blackpill, a visit to Clyne Valley Country Park (SS 6191) can be rewarding. Lying behind the Woodman car park, the valley winds its way up towards Fairwood Common. A series of footpaths follow the route of the former railway line and provides some excellent viewing spots. There is a display board indicating potential walks. A variety of woodland species can be seen. Lesser Spotted Woodpecker has been recorded in the past, as has Willow Tit. It is a good spot to search for migrant passerines.

A visit to Mumbles is recommended. In winter, check the struts beneath Mumbles Pier and the Lifeboat slipway for Purple Sandpipers. They are often seen in the company of Turnstones. In summer a breeding colony of Kittiwakes is active. Skuas sometimes enter the bay on passage; Pomarine, Arctic and Great have all been seen. Manx Shearwaters and Storm Petrels are occasionally seen close inshore during sea-watches at Mumbles Head. In winter check the bay for divers and grebes. The former are not very common although there can be many Great Crested Grebes present. Black Terns have occurred on a number of occasions, Sandwich, Common, Arctic and Little Terns are regular on both spring and autumn passage. Rare terns have included Whiskered, Caspian and Royal.

Oystercatchers – Alan Rosney

40 - OXWICH (SS 5087)

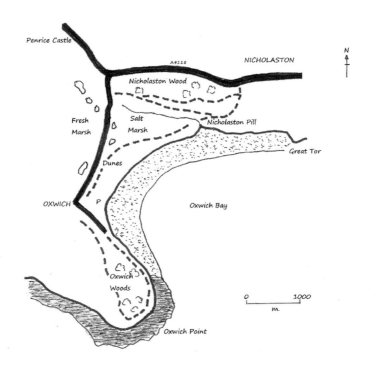

Access

Take the A4118, the main road west from Swansea through south Gower. Leave the A road via a left turn at Penrice Castle (SS 502884) and take the Oxwich road. This narrow road drops steeply downhill past the Castle. It then cuts through the freshwater marsh. For much of its length it follows the boundary between marsh and sand dunes. There is a large car park next to the beach with some facilities. There is a car parking fee.

Parts of the reserve are wheelchair accessible, especially around the car park. Elsewhere however it would mean using the rather narrow and often busy metalled road. This beach is very popular in the summer months and as a consequence there can be quite lengthy hold ups on the access road.

When to visit

Any time of year.

The scenery here is stunning and the bird watching can be very rewarding, although it must be said that it is not as good as it used to be. Recent reed cutting and water level management will help rejuvenate the reserve, hopefully returning it to its former glory.

Oxwich Bay, the largest of the Gower bays, stretches westwards from Three Cliff Bay for approximately 4 kilometres. The dunes trap an extensive area of salt-marsh, freshwater marsh and lagoons, all of which drain to the sea by way of Nicholaston Pill. The dunes show various stages of succession, from the embryonic dunes of the shoreline, the erosion systems and blowouts of the seaward faces, through to the oldest dunes where trees such as Birch and Oak have become established. There are many fine plants to be found here, including rarities such as the Welsh Gentian and a maritime variety of the Round-leaved Wintergreen. Numerous orchids are to be found in May and June. Some of the other plants you might encounter are marsh specialists such as Marsh Cinquefoil, Water Dock, Bog Pimpernel, Marsh Bedstraw, Marsh Horsetail and Marsh Helleborine. Oxwich is home to some unusual white forms of otherwise common plants including Dovesfoot Cranesbill, Restharrow and Common Centaury. This is also one of the few places in Glamorgan where Marbled White butterflies may be seen. Several beetle species are likely to be encountered including the handsome strandline beetle, Nebria complanata.

For the bird watcher, the fens and marshes are of the greatest interest. They were originally reclaimed in the 16th century and for over 300 years provided rich summer grazing. Fish ponds dug in the early 19th century still remain. The largest, of some 7.2 hectares, is aptly named Serpentine Broad. The reed bed extends for some 40 hectares, one of the largest areas of this habitat in south-west Britain. Fifteen species of dragonfly and damselfly have been recorded and plants such as Marestail, Common Bladderwort, Flowering Rush, Bogbean and Marsh Marigold thrive here.

In winter, sea-watching can be productive. The best place to scan the bay is undoubtedly from the main car park. This area is slightly elevated and can give good views. In winter, divers, grebes and sea duck can be expected. Scan the rocks for Oystercatcher, Turnstone and Purple Sandpiper. Sanderling might be seen scurrying up and down the beach.

Venturing from the car park, several walks can be undertaken. Footpaths run to both east and west. The best time to undertake these walks is in the early morning, as the beach area can get crowded later in the day. The most rewarding route, from a bird watching point of view, is to the east. This path winds through the dunes and along the edge of the salt-marsh and reed bed to Nicholaston Pill, whilst the western path leads you in to the woods on the headland.

For the eastern walk, leave the car park and follow the footpath through the sand dunes. Here species such as Linnet, Stonechat, Green Woodpecker and Reed Bunting are likely. Where scrub has invaded the dunes there should be common woodland birds, plus warblers such as Willow Warbler and Chiffchaff. There are areas of Alder and Willow Carr that are worth checking. Grey Heron breed in small numbers. A small heronry has been established, having moved from its former site at Penrice in 2003. By skirting the reed bed there is the chance of seeing Reed, Sedge and Cetti's Warblers. In winter the Nicholaston Pill has Green Sandpiper and Kingfisher and in summer, hirundines hawk for insects over the reeds. Oxwich regularly gets very early hirundine records, as migrants feed up before continuing on their journey north. Check out the hirundine flocks late in the season as Hobbies may be hunting.

There are several river crossings leading in to Nicholaston Woods. A pleasant woodland path skirts the reed bed. The path eventually leads back to the road. Its elevated position means there are good views of the marsh. Nicholaston Woods are host to many common woodland species. Once at the road, turn left, down the hill, doubling back to the starting point. On the right at the bottom of the hill an area of open water can be viewed. Several duck species can be found here in winter, as well as the ubiquitous Coot and Moorhen. Otters have been seen on this stretch of water. It was here that Glamorgan's only Savi's Warbler was found in May 1987.

One bird that most birders hope to see at Oxwich is the Bittern. It is many years since booming was heard, however they are now almost annual winter visitors, particularly during cold snaps.

Little Egret is becoming more regular, as the species continues its spread northwards through the British Isles. Several scarce members of the heron family have been noted here, including Purple Heron. There have been no recent records however. Cormorants also come to fish from their colonies further west in Gower and are often seen perching in the trees. A recent addition to the reserve list is the group of 10 - 20 Greylag Geese that first began visiting the site in 2002.

When walking along the road, check the reed bed on the right. Bearded Tits were recorded in 1970s and 80s. They were assumed to have bred, as birds were still present in late July and a juvenile was caught and ringed. As the species appears to be spreading west, they may return. It is almost certain that Water Rails nest here and they can certainly be heard throughout the year. Woodcock also inhabit these damp areas. Small numbers of Black-headed Gulls have nested in the past and they still occur in most months. Marsh Harriers regularly pass this way on migration and one or two may spend the summer in Glamorgan. Osprey may also make a stop-over, although they are more at home on the North Gower marshes.

Shoveler, Pochard and Mallard have all bred in the past. Proof of breeding is quite difficult, as there is very restricted viewing of the open water of the marsh. Unfortunately the former hide is now unusable. Garganey are scarce but regular passage migrants in the early spring. Wader records tend to be few due to the lack of muddy margins. The drumming displays of Snipe in spring are now a thing of the past, though many come to winter here, while the passage of too many feet on the beach has meant the end of breeding Ringed Plovers.

An alternative walk is to the west along the limestone headland at the western end of the bay. Take the path through the woods which hugs the side of the bay. It eventually leads to Oxwich Church, once the site of the largest rookery in Gower. Unfortunately this died out, largely as a result of Dutch Elm disease and breeding ceased in 1992. By continuing to the point, good views of the bay can be obtained. The sheltered eastern side attracts feeding sea birds, especially in winter. In the woods, typical woodland species might be encountered. Look out for tits, Treecreeper, Nuthatch etc. All three woodpeckers have occurred and Yellow-browed Warblers were recorded here in autumn 2003 and 2005.

41 - WHITEFORD POINT (SS 4595)

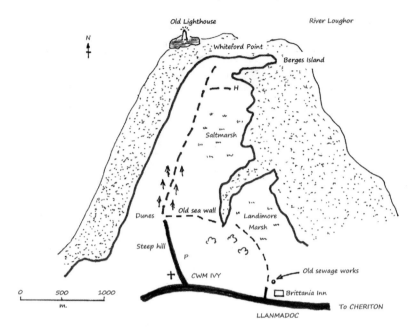

Access

Take the north Gower road B4295, by-passing Penclawdd, Crofty and Wernffrwd. From Old Walls, head for Cheriton and Llanmadoc. There is a car park in the field on the right for which an honesty box is provided. Spectacular views of the point can be had from here. The walk to the point is approximately 2-3 kilometres. Allow an hour or two to reach the point. It is over variable terrain, including tarmac, marshy ground and sand dunes. From the car park, walk down the steep hill. At the bottom of the hill, take the path that runs through the line of conifers on to the open marsh land. Follow the long curved path around the edge of the dunes towards Berges Island. This path is often flooded – wellingtons are essential. Don't be tempted to take a short cut across the marsh as it is potentially very dangerous. There are no facilities nearby. It is not recommended to undertake this walk in poor weather, as there is very little shelter. Wheelchair access is impossible.

An alternative walk down to the marshes is along the old sea wall. Either start from Frog Lane, Llanmadoc, alongside the

Brittania Inn. or take the path through the Betty Church/Cwm Ivy reserve. The entrance to this reserve is via a gate on the right hand side of the steep road down to the marshes. It is marked with an orange and white notice. Examination of the old sewage works is often worthwhile as both Firecrest and Chiffchaff have over-wintered recently. This path can get very muddy. The Lucas WTSWW Reserve (SS 447933) also lies adjacent to the Brittania Inn.

When to visit

This promontory jutting out into the Loughor Estuary is one of the premier sites in Glamorgan. For bird watching, it is at its best in the winter, although it is a beautiful area that is worth visiting at any time of year. It is recommended to be in position on the point just after high water, as the tide recedes to reveal the first feeding areas for waders and before divers, grebes and duck move too far off-shore. Choose a period of spring tides, especially if planning to use the hide at Berges Island.

The Burry Inlet is an internationally important area for wildfowl. It contains one of the largest areas of grazed salt-marsh in Britain. Behind this the massive dune system of Whiteford Burrows, extends 3.2 kilometres northwards from the village of Cwm Ivy and Llandimore Marsh. The burrows are owned by the National Trust and much of it is now a National Nature Reserve, managed by the Countryside Council for Wales. Apart from the birds, there are many other things to see at Whiteford, including Dune Gentian, Moonwort, Yellow Birds nest, Bird's-foot Trefoil, Lady's Bedstraw and Sea Pansies. Rare insects and Otters have also been recorded.

Large flocks of Brent Geese, Shelduck, Wigeon, Teal, Pintail, Oystercatcher, Knot, Curlew, Redshank, Turnstone, Bar-tailed Godwit and Dunlin may be encountered in winter. A very special sight is that of flocks of waders wheeling across the marsh. Good numbers of Snipe winter on the saltings. The marshy area just beyond the conifer belt is particularly good for Jack Snipe. Keep an eye out for Peregrine and Merlin hunting over the marshes. The presence of Raven is often indicated by their 'cronking' calls echoing across the landscape. Both Spotted Redshank and Green Sandpiper over-winter, while Whimbrel occur on spring passage. This is one of the few areas in Glamorgan where Eider are regular. They often rest on the sand banks at low water. A fairly common sight here are Red-breasted Mergansers, which can be seen in small numbers in almost all months. Common Scoters are present in winter, just west of the point and Velvet Scoter are a possibility. Both Long-tailed Duck and Goldeneye might be seen. Great Crested Grebes should be seen throughout the year, especially in the Llanrhidian area, with numbers rising to around a hundred in the autumn.

Some of the 'special' birds of the area are the smaller grebes. Up to eight Slavonian Grebes spend the winter off Whiteford. The best way to see them is to get into position on the point, at the top of a falling tide, watching as they drift out to sea. Black-necked Grebes do occur but in smaller numbers. A walk to the point may be worthwhile. The flat rocks often have several wader species present. Large numbers of Oystercatchers may be joined by Turnstones, Ringed Plovers, Dunlin and Purple Sandpipers. From here, it is possible to see all three diver species and Scaup are also a possibility. Cormorants are always to be found on the old abandoned lighthouse.

Black-headed Gulls occur throughout the year. The handful present in early summer are joined by many more later in the season. By August, thousands can be present, even though most will move on. One should check for Mediterranean Gulls amongst the Black-heads. Common Gulls follow a similar pattern to the Black-headed, though in smaller numbers. Kittiwakes occasionally move into the estuary and are more frequently seen off the point. On passage, small numbers of Sandwich and Common Terns occur.

Whilst the main interest is undoubtedly the waders and wildfowl, a good variety of passerines may also be seen. The conifer belt is one of the most reliable sites in the county to see Crossbills, Also in this area are Coal Tits, Goldcrests and on occasions, Firecrest. Linnets, Reed Buntings, Goldfinches and Stonechats frequent the invasive scrub on the dunes and Black Redstarts have been seen in the dune area. Shore Lark, a very rare bird in Glamorgan, has been recorded here three times, the last being in 2002-3. Another very rare species, a Bluethroat, was found in October 2001. Brambling and Snow Bunting are distinct possibilities in winter. Look for woodpeckers and winter thrushes in the deciduous woods of Cwm Ivy. A Yellow-browed Warbler was found in 2005. On returning to the car park, check the hedgerows for Marsh Tit.

42 - LLANRHIDIAN MARSH (SS 4893)

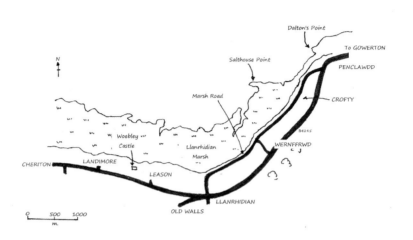

Access

The B4295 at Penclawdd runs along the shoreline and provides many good viewing points for this section of the upper estuary, as does Salthouse Point (SS 523956). An old causeway used to provide access to the point but there have been access problems recently. An alternative access point is via the Crofty Industrial Estate. Park by the 'cockle factory' and walk west to the edge of the salt-marsh. Try to find an elevated spot and use a telescope to scan across the area. There are some old wartime earth mounds from which it is relatively easy to scan the marsh. Beyond Crofty, a minor road bears off the B4295 and follows the edge of the saltings for about 4 kilometres, until it rejoins the main road in Llanrhidian. To the west lies some 6 kilometres of salt-marsh. Wheelchair users should be able to scan from the roadside.
[Note that the marsh road can get flooded when tides are high].

When to visit

Late winter is undoubtedly the best time to visit. Some 'good' birds turn up on passage.

This is an extensive rushy salt-marsh area which is dotted with pools and crossed by many inter-tidal streams. In winter, there

121

is a good chance of seeing raptors such as Hen Harrier, Merlin, Peregrine, Short-eared and Barn Owls. The best time to visit is just before dusk when the harriers are gathering and the owls are becoming active. Choose any vantage point on the marsh road and you should be rewarded with some spectacular bird watching as the raptors hunt over the marsh. A telescope is recommended. In autumn, this has proved to be the best place in Glamorgan to see Osprey. They are almost annual and tend to stay for a few days. Check the posts on the marsh.

Osprey – Alan Rosney

Golden Plover can be seen on the shorter turf towards Crofty village. Other waders can also be seen very close to the road. Common Sandpipers have over-wintered here and Green Sandpipers are possible. Little Egret are often seen on the marsh, sometimes in considerable numbers. 80 were seen going to roost below Woebley Castle in December 2008. Spoonbills have also been recorded. Some very rare visitors have graced this area in the past; a Desert Wheatear was at Penclawdd in November 1992, a Roller was at Welsh Moor in August 2007 and a Golden Oriole visited the area in May 2008.

There are two local WTSWW reserves in the area; Hambury Woods, Landimore (SS 472929) where Marsh Tit has been recorded plus many commoner woodland species and Llanrhidian Hill (SS 495922) which has grassland species.

43 - WORM'S HEAD
The Worm (SS 3887) and Rhossili Down (SS 4290)

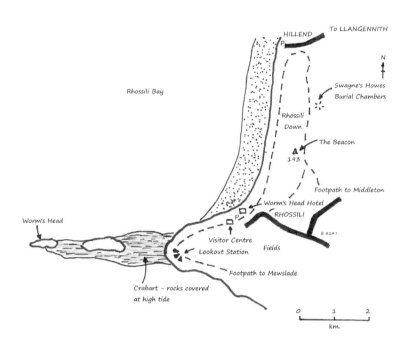

Access

Take the South Gower Road (A4118). At Scurlage, turn right on to the B4247 and continue for approximately 5 kilometres. The B4247 ends in Rhossili village, where there is a large pay and display car park. A wide cliff-top path leads south-west to the head. The path is approximately 1 kilometre long and is fairly flat.

Worm's Head, Rhossili Down and the whole 10 kilometres of cliff stretching eastwards to Port Eynon is part of a nature reserve managed by the WTSWW, the National Trust and the Countryside Council for Wales, who all have holdings here. There is a coastal footpath leading to Port Eynon. This is arguably one of the best sections of cliff coast in the whole of Wales, offering a fine vantage point. There are several facilities on site with toilets in the car park, as well as in the pub. Wheelchair access would be quite difficult here.

Urban sites

Cardiff Bay with the city in the background. The wetland reserve is centre right

Cosmeston west lake, a former quarry site which is now a nature reserve

Some recent rarities

Black-winged Stilt at Kenfig NNR

Spotted Sandpiper at Lisvane reservoir

Whiskered Tern at Kenfig NNR

Red-necked Phalarope at Ogmore Castle

When to visit

It can be good at any time of year. Visit in spring for breeding birds. Winter is best for sea-watching.

[Note that anyone wishing to visit Worm's Head should consult the tide tables. Enquire in Rhossili as to times or telephone the coastguard if in any doubt. Cross as the tide begins to recede from the rocky causeway and you should then have a window allowing approximately five hours on the Worm. Note that wind strength and direction can reduce this window. Give yourself plenty of time to return. There have been fatalities in the past, with unwary visitors getting cut off by the rising tide. Visitors are requested not to visit the Outer Head from 1st March until 31st August to avoid disturbance of breeding seabirds].

The Worm lies at the southern extremity of Gower. The narrow grass-topped promontory is connected to the mainland by an extensive rocky causeway which is revealed at low tide. Access to the Worm is possible for several hours either side of low water.

The head is some 14.8 hectares in extent and comprises four small hills, rising like a dragon's serrated back. The name 'Worm' in Norse means dragon or serpent. Much of the headland is covered in Red Fescue, this providing ample food for the sheep that graze the table-top plateau of the Inner Worm. Other maritime plants include Spring Squill, Sea Beet, Golden and Rock Samphire, Tree Mallow, Rock Sea-lavender, Sea Storksbill and Buckshorn Plantain.

The scenery here is spectacular; indeed the raised beach of Rhossili is featured in many tourist postcards and brochures. The ancient field systems of the Worm should definitely be checked in the autumn. Large numbers of finches and larks are present in these weedy fields. A footpath runs from the car park, south-west from the village through these fields. Look for Yellowhammer, Linnet, Tree Sparrow, Reed Bunting etc. These birds tend to gather in autumn and winter to feed on the weed seeds and stubble. Rarities have included Ortolan, Wryneck and Lapland Bunting and a Corncrake was flushed from this area in 2007. Wheatear may be seen in spring and summer and in winter Golden Plovers sometimes gather here.

In 1991 Dartford Warblers started appearing and pairs were discovered breeding at two or three sites. With recent mild winters and large expanses of suitable cliff-top habitat, this species is spreading along the south Gower coast.

After checking the fields explore the headland. From the car park, follow the footpath alongside the stone wall, down towards the promontory. The closely cropped turf attracts Chough to this section of cliff-top. They first bred here in 1991 and have steadily expanded their range. Look for raptors as Peregrine and Kestrel are likely. The crossing to Worm's Head is reached at the cliff edge. The end of the head beyond the Coastguard Station is a good spot from which to scan the flat rocks and sea area of Crabart. The coastal bushes often have Whitethroat in summer.

The seabird colonies on the Worm are regionally quite important. Kittiwakes were formerly numerous. In common with colonies elsewhere, there has been a recent decline. They ceased breeding here in 2003. Guillemots and Razorbills both nest in very small numbers, although the breeding sites are only visible from the sea. Puffins were first recorded at Worm's Head in 1848 but they are now rarely seen. [Note that boat trips leave from either Mumbles or Port Eynon, giving opportunities to view breeding auks, seals etc. Contact: *Gower Coast Adventures* on 07866250440 – website address www.gowercoastadventures.co.uk].

The large gulls have had mixed fortunes. Lesser Black-backed Gulls once nested in small numbers but they have now ceased to do so, probably the result of increased visitor numbers and predation by foxes. Herring Gulls were once numerous but now only a small colony survives. Great Black-backed Gulls have followed the same pattern, with only sporadic breeding noted. Other breeding species include several pairs of Fulmar, Shag, Meadow and Rock Pipits and Jackdaws.

Passage waders frequent the rocky causeway whatever the season, even at the height of the summer, Oystercatchers and Turnstones should be present. From August onwards, look for visiting Purple Sandpipers. They are easily overlooked.

As stated earlier, Worm's Head and the cliffs can be good for sea-watching. The Carmarthen Bay scoter flock often moves close to land. Sometimes sizeable numbers congregate in Rhossili Bay. Look for the white wing flashes of Velvet Scoter, as they sometimes associate with their commoner cousins. Surf Scoters have also been recorded on a couple of occasions. Other sea duck, such as Eider, can also be seen and divers and grebes are regularly recorded off the head in the winter. In certain weather conditions and particularly following strong south-west winds, Manx Shearwaters, Mergansers, Gannets, terns and auks get pushed high into Carmarthen Bay and are seen off the Head. Occasionally Storm-Petrels get blown in close to shore. Very occasionally Long-tailed Ducks appear in the bay.

An alternative walk is on to Rhossili Down (SS 4290). It is ideally situated for migratory birds to make landfall. From the main car park, walk past St. Mary's Church, through a gate, crossing the small bridge on to the footpath. Walk north along the cliff–top, keeping a look out for Kestrel and Peregrine. The path is quite steep in parts. There is a small car park alongside the Hillend Caravan Park. From here turn south towards the Beacon. National Trust signs point to Rhossili Down. The Gorse in this area can hold interesting species and Chough are often seen flying over. Species such as Dotterel and Ring Ouzel have been recorded in the past, although not recently. A Common Rosefinch was discovered on the Down in November 2004. Once past the Beacon, one can return to the main car park or take a detour to Middleton.

Dotterel – Colin Richards

44 - MEWSLADE (SS 4287)

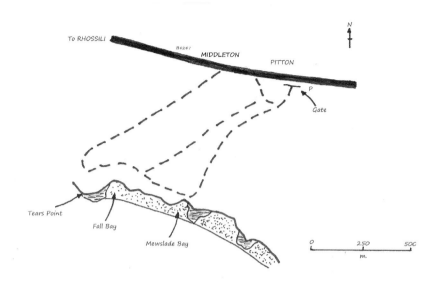

Access

On the B4247 towards Rhossili, at Pitton, take the only left hand turn in the village. The road bears round to the left. From here, go through the field gateway to the car park. There is an honesty box on the gate post for the parking fee. Walk out of the car park and turn left, bearing right around the old barns and garages. Look for a gate to the right of the green tin barn. This leads out along a narrow track towards the beach. Wheelchair access would be impossible.

When to visit

Good at any time but recommended in spring and autumn.

The north-east to south-west orientation of the Mewslade valley means that it acts like a funnel for migrant birds. Many visitors merely 'bird' the valley but a circular walk can be productive. The path from the farm down to the sea is initially fairly level but it can get muddy. Lower down valley the terrain gets rather rocky nearer to the sea. Check the stone walls and outcrops for Little Owl. Passing through the gate out of the woods, continue down hill towards the beach. For the circular route take the cliff path to the right. This path leads towards Fall Bay. Arriving at the headland above Fall Bay, look for a set of wooden steps that lead on to the farmland on your right. In autumn the weedy fields hereabouts have held Woodlark, plus Ring Ouzels have been fairly regular. Once up in the fields, take the stile some 30 metres ahead and bear left along the field boundaries on to a farm track. This eventually emerges at the main road in the village of Middleton. From here turn right down the main road for 600 metres in order to return to the car park.

The area is perhaps best known for the discovery of the Red Lady of Paviland, a Paleolithic skeleton found in 1823. It was subsequently identified as a man. As well as Paviland Cave, there are a number of other caves along this stretch of coast. The sea-sculpted rocks are particularly impressive. The diversity of habitats; woods, Gorse, Bracken, quarry, rocky shore, beach and farmland encourages a wide variety of bird species. These range from common woodland birds such as tits and finches, warblers and woodpeckers through to farmland specialists like Yellowhammer, Stock Dove, Linnet and Grey Partridge. Stonechat may be found in the Gorse. Overhead Chough are regular and Raven, Buzzard and Peregrine might be seen.

A scan of the sea might yield some of the same species as encountered on Worm's Head e.g. Shag, Fulmar, Scoter and possibly divers and auks. The site has gained a reputation for turning up some 'good' birds in recent years. Some of the scarcer birds that have been encountered include Short-eared Owl and Firecrest. Real rarities have included Yellow-browed Warbler in October 2004, Little Bunting in November 2005, Icterine Warbler in September 2006 and Common Rosefinch in October 2007. There was also a Pallas's Warbler at Middleton in October 2006.

If you have time, it is worth checking the gardens to the north of the B4247; the roving tit flocks often 'carry' migrant warblers. Nitten Field (SS 423875) on the western shoulder of the valley is also worth exploring. It is being managed for birds, with a variety of crops, such as sunflowers, being sown to attract birds. Ringing is regularly undertaken here.

Another site worth exploring is Deborah's Hole WTSWW reserve at Pilton (SS 435862). This former quarry has calcareous grassland, heath and scrub habitat and affords views of the Knave, an off-shore stack with attendant seabirds. It was here that the first breeding Fulmars on Gower were discovered in 1955. On a clear day the Island of Lundy can be seen far out in the Bristol Channel.

45 - PORT EYNON (SS 4784)

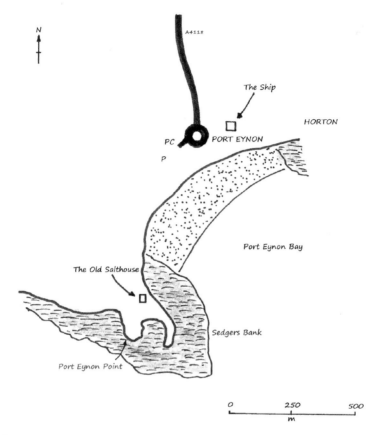

Access

Take the A4118 south Gower road to Scurlage. Continue on the A road, dropping down a steep hill. The road in to the village of Port Eynon is quite narrow. There is a large car park next to the beach. There are shops, toilets and a pub in the village. There is a regular bus service from Swansea to Port Eynon. The areas around the car parks are accessible for wheelchair users, however the headland is not.

When to visit

This is the most southerly point on Gower and is primarily a sea-watching site. There are two peak periods; late July/early August and January/February. Depending on tides, early morning is the best time to visit. Strong south-westerlies are recommended.

Much of the area is within the Wildlife Trust Reserve (13.4 hectares). It is made up of sea cliffs, limestone rocks, grazed grassland, heath, Gorse and some old quarries. Rabbits keep the turf well grazed with the result that plants such as Sea Campion, Thrift, Spring Squill and Wild Clary thrive.

Check the bushes adjacent to the coastal path between the car park and the old salt house for Stonechat, Linnet, Goldfinch and other passerines. These can hold good numbers of migrants, when conditions are right. Thrushes often gather to strip berries from the bushes. Peregrine, Buzzard and Kestrel can also be encountered and Chough might be seen in the fields.

For sea-watching, a telescope is essential. Beware as the rocks on the point get covered at high tide and they can also become very slippery. Check out the rocks for Turnstone, Curlew, Oystercatcher, Grey Plover, Rock Pipit etc. A late July/early August visit might bring good numbers of Manx Shearwaters and Gannets. Given strong winds, Storm-Petrels and skuas can get driven relatively close to the shore. This is one of the few points on the Glamorgan coast where terns are fairly regular, with Sandwich being the commonest. In winter, divers and sea duck might be present and Purple Sandpipers should be on the rocks.

Nearby there are two other reserves that might be worth a visit - Overton Mere (SS 464848) and Overton Cliffs (SS 459849). Both are primarily known for their flora but the cliffs have breeding Herring Gulls and Jackdaws.

Eider – Bob Mitchell

46 - CWM CLYDACH RSPB (SN 6703)

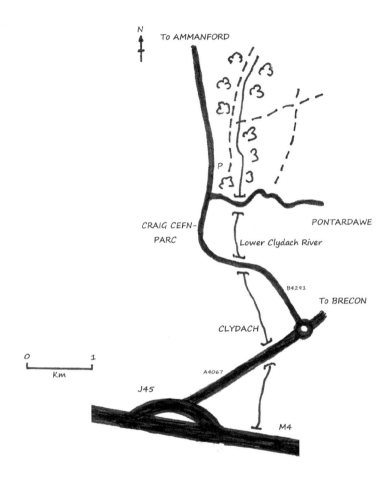

Access

Leave the M4 at junction 45 and take the A4067 Brecon road for approximately 3 kilometres. At the roundabout, turn left on the B4291 towards Clydach. In Clydach, continue along the B4291 (Vardre Road) towards Craig Cefn-Parc. Beyond the residential area the road dips downhill. Continue on this road looking for the New Inn on the right hand side. The entrance to the reserve is just over the bridge on the right. The reserve is open at all times but check the opening times for the car park. The path from the car park to a point at approximately SN 676034 is suitable for wheelchair use but beyond this point the terrain becomes uneven. Sturdy footwear is recommended. For those using the bus, there is an hourly bus service from Swansea to Craig Cefn-Parc which stops at the reserve. For further information, call the RSPB offices in Cardiff on 02920 353000.

When to visit

The reserve is probably best in spring (March through to May) although there is something of interest at other times of year. You may visit at any time of day, although early morning is recommended.

The RSPB Cwm Clydach reserve lies 11.2 kilometres north of the centre of Swansea. It is situated in the narrow valley of the same name. The reserve is a good example of upland Welsh woodland habitat. Following an initial acquisition of 49 hectares, further sections of woodland have been acquired by the RSPB. Today a major reserve of 87 hectares exists, relatively close to a large urban centre.

Three hundred years of coal mining, albeit on a small scale, have left their mark on the valley. The mines are a now a distant memory, although the old tramway still functions as the main visitor trail through the southern part of the reserve.

The path from the car park skirts the river, giving excellent opportunities to observe a range of common woodland species, as well as Dipper and Grey Wagtail on the river. Marsh Tit and Spotted Flycatcher have been seen along this stretch. At approximately SN 676034, a bridge over the river gives the choice of following routes either to the west or the east of the river. Both routes continue through woodland. The path to the west eventually passes fields and the one to the east leads to a boardwalk, surrounded by an expanse of Bracken. Both routes ultimately end at Pont Llechart Bridge (accessed from the eastern route via the farm road).

It is best to pause at regular intervals to see what is about, always keeping an eye on the sky as a number of the Cwm Clydach species (Raven, Buzzard, Peregrine etc) are observed in flight over the reserve. The fields and hills on the fringes of the valley can hold Tree Pipits, Whinchats and Wheatears in summer.

The southern stretch of the reserve is very good for seeing common woodland species but it can be rather inconsistent for observing scarcer species such as Lesser Spotted Woodpecker, Wood Warbler and Pied Flycatcher. For these species, it is recommended to follow the path north from Pont Llechart Bridge (SN 687045) for 1-2 km. The terrain is rather uneven here. The initial stages of the southern part of the reserve nicely combine birding with a relaxed stroll. The northern section is more strenuous.

In winter Snipe and Woodcock are recorded in small numbers and there are usually Fieldfares, Redwings, Siskin and Redpoll. This reserve requires some perseverance to observe all the possible species, so allow a few hours. Beyond the reserve, the road climbs on to higher ground with a picnic site at SN 668068, overlooking the Lliw Reservoirs. Goosanders tend to gather here in winter.

The scrubby areas on the fringes of the main woodland can hold Whitethroat, Yellowhammer, Whinchat and Tree Pipit. Further along the road the high moors hold Meadow Pipit, Linnet and Wheatear. Curlew and Lapwing have bred in this area in the past.

Goosanders – Paul Parsons

47 – THE LLIW RESERVOIRS
Lower Lliw (SN 6403) and Upper Lliw (SN 6606)

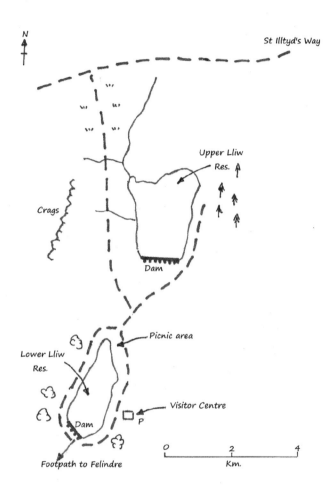

Access

To get to the Lliw Valley Reservoirs, leave the M4 at Junction 46 and take the road (Heol Llangyfelach) towards Felindre village (SS 6302) After approximately an 80 metre stretch of road, that is effectively single file, you immediately reach a sharp right-hand turn by a group of houses. Here the road starts to drop downhill towards Felindre village. Take a right hand turn (Heol Penfidy) and follow the signs to the reservoir entrance. The gated entrance appears suddenly on the left about 50 metres after a sharp right hand bend. There is a 1 km access road to the car park. The tarmac road leading from the car park goes all the way up to Upper Lliw Reservoir. This provides a linear route along which you can stop and return at any point. Wheelchair users can utilise these well maintained roads. Be aware of occasional vehicles using this road. The local residents, for example, use this road to access their property. **[Note that the gate at the entrance opens at 8 a.m. and closes at 7 p.m. To check opening times call 01792 799479].**

When to visit

The area is at its best in spring and summer, although there is generally something of interest throughout the year. An early morning visit is recommended.

The Lower and Upper Lliw Reservoirs are situated just to the north of the city of Swansea in quiet, relaxing countryside surroundings. There are good facilities with car parking, toilets, café and an office that issues fishing permits. There are a variety of walks for everyone, ranging from a gentle stroll around the perimeter of the reservoirs, through to a 6 kilometre route which is suitable for wheelchairs and pushchairs, or for the really energetic there is an open moorland route of over 15 kilometres.

Birds are attracted by the diversity of habitats available within this relatively compact area. These include reservoirs, deciduous and coniferous woodland, farmland, mountains and moorland. Over 80 species of birds have been recorded here. There is the potential to observe over 50 species in a day, particularly in the spring.

The circular walk around the Lower Lliw Reservoir involves taking a left turn at the wooden gate, just before the end of the woodland. The path goes down some steep steps, crosses a bridge over the stream and skirts the reservoir along an uneven path. Ultimately the path bears left over the dam and returns to the car park. Bushes either side of the path leading from the car park can be good for finches and thrushes. The path then gives one the opportunity to view the water and adjoining fields. There is the chance of seeing Whitethroat in the bushes on the left. The path then bears left; the area on the right can be good for warblers, including Chiffchaff, Grasshopper Warbler and Willow Warblers.

Next there is a stretch of woodland. This area has many of the common woodland birds such as finches, tits and warblers. It is worth checking the area around the house. The right hand side is good for Goldcrest, Blackcap, Garden Warbler, various tits, Nuthatch and Spotted Flycatcher. Another site for Spotted Flycatcher is in the area around the wooden gate on the circular walk. Below you is the Lower Lliw reservoir. The birds here obviously vary with the season. In winter you can scan the water for the opportunity of seeing Goosander. Dipper and Grey Wagtail are present for most of the year and Common Sandpiper occasionally drop in on passage.

The path leaves the woodland and enters the more open terrain of mountains, moorland and gorse. Willow Warblers, Yellowhammer and Cuckoo are likely nearby. Ravens and raptors may be present. The path curves right by an old quarry which is an excellent site for Stock Dove and Redstart.

Yellowhammer – Bob Mitchell

Continue along the path for the Upper Lliw Reservoir. Willow Warbler, Grasshopper Warbler, Whitethroat, Reed Bunting, Stonechat, Whinchat and Meadow Pipit may be observed along the way. The quarry to the left can hold raptors and the crags often have

Wheatear in spring. The Upper Lliw Reservoir generally holds similar species to those found on the lower reservoir.

The coniferous woodland to the right of the reservoir has many of the common woodland birds. In addition there is the possibility of seeing Crossbills, especially early in the year. The Lliw Reservoirs offer relatively easy access to a great range of habitats and bird species and consistently delivers an extremely enjoyable and rewarding bird watching experience.

Area 8 : THE VALE OF GLAMORGAN

Site 48 Aberthaw
Site 49 Cosmeston Lakes
Site 50 Lavernock Point
Site 51 Southerndown
Site 52 Ogmore
Site 53 Nash Point

Golden Plover – Paul Parsons

48 – ABERTHAW
East Aberthaw (ST 0366) and West Aberthaw (ST 0266)

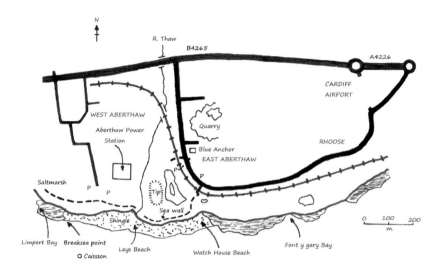

Access

    This long site lies to the south of the B4265 Cardiff Airport to St. Athan road. It can be considered in two parts; east and west. Both are linked by the substantial concrete sea wall that doubles as a footpath. The two parts are separated and dominated by Aberthaw Power Station and its ash tip. Much of the site is private; however most of it can be viewed from the footpaths or the sea wall.

    East Aberthaw is a WTSWW reserve. It can be accessed from two points. Park in one of two lay-bys, just short of the East Aberthaw sign and follow the private road across the railway bridge. There are several footpaths that criss-cross the site. Alternatively, park in the car park opposite the Blue Anchor pub. From here follow Well Lane, which leads downhill and under the railway line. A path leads off to the left.

    West Aberthaw can be accessed from the B4265. There is a turn just after the garage. Immediately turn right through the village and then left towards the Leys Beach. At the end of this lane are two car parks, one behind and one to the left of the only house. At this point the sea wall is once again obvious. Following it on the landward side eventually takes you back to East Aberthaw. Wheelchair users will not be able to access East Aberthaw but could possibly access some parts of the West.

When to visit
Can be productive at any time of year

Aberthaw is situated on the coast between Cardiff Wales International Airport and the MoD facility at St Athan. The Aberthaw Power Station dominates the western area. The ash tip (which is now quite well grassed) to the east covers what was formerly a superb lagoon area that contributed strongly to the formidable list of rarities that have appeared at the site. In the 1970's Spotted Crake, Temminck's Stint and Least Sandpiper were recorded. Only a remnant of this area now remains, however the bushy habitat that surrounds it still has a reputation for holding rarities. Wryneck, Hoopoe, Golden Oriole and Woodchat Shrike have all been found here. The pool has Little Grebe, Coot, Moorhen and Water Rail. It has also hosted some rare waders and ducks. This site is at the southernmost tip of Wales (Rhoose Point, just to the east of Aberthaw is actually the most southerly point) and consequently is attractive for migrant birds.

As stated in the access section, East Aberthaw is best reached via the footpath over the railway line. The ruin of a former lime works dominates this section. The bushes can attract migrants as well as some breeding birds. Lesser and Common Whitethroat may be found in the scrub below the lime works. The former is more often heard than seen however. Just below the bushes the sea wall should be obvious. Linnets are often found on or near the sea wall.

From the wall it is possible to scan the salt-marsh, shingle and sandy beach. Waders and gulls may be present and Shelduck are fairly regular here. An Avocet, a rare bird in Glamorgan, has been recorded here once. Just to the east are some low cliffs which are worth scanning for breeding birds. To the west, the bushes to the rear of the pool and the ash tip are worth investigation. The latter has been one of the few areas in Glamorgan where one can see Grey Partridge **[Note that the tip is on private land and access is forbidden]**.

Those wishing to visit West Aberthaw along the coastal fringe and the river can do so by walking behind the sea wall and heading west. Alternatively return to the car and drive west, passing the Blue Anchor pub on your right and the cement works on your left. On the right there is a large quarry (which is not visible from the road) that may be viewed from the bridge. There are also some lagoons that occasionally hold duck. Parking may be a problem.

Limpert Bay usually has gulls and waders. Behind the fence is a good spot to search for Black Redstarts in winter. They have been seen in most recent winters. Breaksea Point can be a good sea-watching point when the winds are from the south-west. From here you can view the concrete caisson structure off-shore. This attracts a lot of gulls. Little Gulls are frequently seen in winter. The Leys beach attracts many wader species and is a good spot to find Eider Duck, a scarce species in the east of the county. Perhaps the 'star' bird found here was the Ivory Gull that appeared following storms in January 1998.

A footpath runs west away from the pebble beach at West Aberthaw. There are scrubby hedgerows here that can be good for migrants at passage times. It can be quite boggy in places.

Hoopoe – Paul Parsons

49 - COSMESTON LAKES (ST 1769)

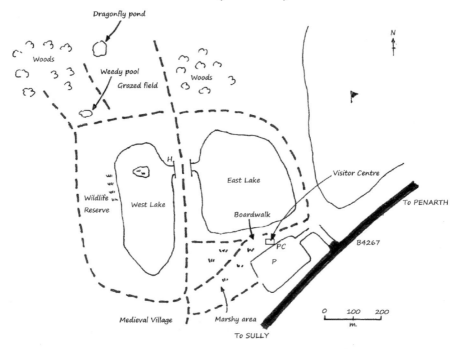

Access

Cosmeston Lakes Country Park can be accessed from the B4267 between Penarth and Sully and is well signposted. There is a large car park by the East Lake, plus an overflow car park on the opposite side of the entrance road. The park can become very crowded at weekends and on bank holidays. It is possible to get away from the crowds. An early morning visit is recommended, before dog walkers and joggers are about. The Visitor Centre provides information and rangers are sometimes present. There is an information board in the car park showing the main paths, which are well surfaced and are wheelchair accessible. Toilet facilities and a cafeteria are available at the Visitor Centre, which is open daily throughout the year. The Park is also home to the Cosmeston Medieval Village. The telephone number of the centre is 02920 701678. For further information go to the Vale of Glamorgan website at www.valeofglamorgan.gov.uk. There is a hide at the northern end of the West Lake.

When to visit

This site can be productive in both spring and winter. Its proximity to the coast attracts occasional rarities.

This site covers 85 hectares, from the Glamorganshire Golf Course in the east, to Cogan Plantation in the west and as far north as Cogan Hall Farm. The lakes were originally limestone quarries that ceased operation in June 1970. Some of the site has SSSI status. The site has two main lakes, covering 25 hectares, numerous small ponds and 25 hectares of woodland. The rest of the park consists of reed bed, marsh, scrub and pasture. The site is best accessed from the car park, through the gate by the information board.

The area in front of the main entrance is where many Swans, gulls and ducks congregate and it provides a good view over the East Lake. The birds here are fairly approachable and can be easily studied. Check the gulls as Ring-billed, Mediterranean and Little have been seen in past winters. Sandwich and Common Terns have both occurred in recent springs. Remarkably a Manx Shearwater was 'wrecked' here after storms in September 1997. From the Visitor Centre, turn left and proceed along the boardwalk. Note that it can be quite slippery.

In winter, the ditches and marshy areas around the Visitor Centre normally hold Water Rails that are more often heard than seen. Recent tape luring surveys have established that Cosmeston probably has the highest density of Water Rails in the east of the county, with 31 being counted in November 2008. The reed beds between the Visitor Centre and the small copse have Reed Warbler, Sedge Warbler and fairly tame Reed Buntings. In summer, Cetti's Warbler has been recorded here and Bearded Tit has occurred on passage. At the end of the boardwalk there is a feeding station, where finch and tit species are usually present. A Woodchat Shrike was near the Medieval Village in May 2002.

Beyond the feeding area the track joins the main footpath through the park. From here to the left there is a loop around the West Lake or a right turn leads up the central causeway. Both lakes may be viewed from the bridge and the West Lake has viewing platforms. Cosmeston often has records of early (and late) hirundines. Swallows and martins feed here prior to continuing their journeys.

In winter the Pochard and Tufted Duck flocks should be checked as Redhead, Ferruginous Ring-necked and Ruddy Ducks have all been found amongst them in recent years. Scaup are regular and in December 2008 a Lesser Scaup, a Glamorgan first, was discovered. (It commuted between here and Cardiff Bay).

.

Breeding birds of the West Lake include Great Crested Grebe, Little Grebe and Mute Swan. A Pied-billed Grebe was found here in 1999. Kingfishers have been seen, both here and at the dragonfly pond. In winter the scrub alongside the path either side of the bridge should be checked for Goldcrest, Firecrest, Chiffchaff and Blackcap.

On the far side of the bridge there is a small wood on the left with a hide on the edge of the water. In winter, the reed bed opposite the hide should be checked for Bittern, Snipe and Water Rail. There are usually Cormorants on the posts in front of the hide. Check them out as sometimes *sinensis* race birds occur. From the main path there are three choices; turn right and return to the car park around the East Lake, go straight on and walk along the lane towards Cogan Hall Farm or take the path that leads around the West Lake towards the woods. The scrub on the left in summer can hold both Common and Lesser Whitethroats. In September 2008 a Wryneck was found near the dragonfly pond.

In winter, Fieldfares and Redwings can often be seen feeding on berries. As the path reaches the brow of the hill you may return to the car park by walking around the West Lake or alternatively turn right and walk into the woods. In summer the woods host many breeding birds including Tawny Owl, Green Woodpecker, Goldcrest, Jay, Blackcap, Willow Warbler and Chiffchaff. Garden Warbler and Marsh Tit bred in the past. There is also a large active Rookery.

At the far end of the woods the path overlooks a water treatment works, which although it is now slightly overgrown, has hosted species such as Teal and Water Rail. Exit the woods and the marshy field straight ahead often has Snipe in winter. From here any of the tracks return to the main footpath and back to the car park.

There is a guided bird walk around the lakes on the third Saturday in each month, led by the Glamorgan Bird Club. Meet in the car park at 9 30 a.m

.50 - LAVERNOCK POINT (ST 1867)

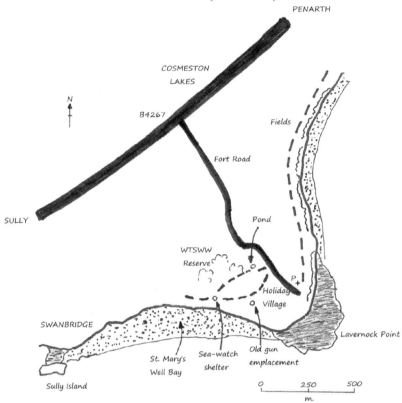

Access

Leave the B4267 Penarth to Barry road at ST 178687 and take the unclassified road, Fort Road, leading directly to the point. There is a brown tourist sign indicating 'Lavernock Point'. Continue along Fort Road, which is quite narrow in parts. Go past the caravan/chalet park on the right hand side. There is a small gravel car park on the left. It is also sometimes possible to park in front of the church at the end of the lane. Unfortunately there are no facilities on site. Wheelchair/scooter users would be able to explore the lanes but the rest of the area is inaccessible,

When to visit

This site is especially good when autumn migration is under way, particularly during August through to October. Spring can also be productive. Early mornings are best.

Lavernock Point sits above the 15 metre high Lias limestone cliffs that are characteristic of the Heritage Coast. It is centrally placed between Penarth and Sully. The habitat is field and hedgerow to the north with a grassland reserve with some scrub to the west. From a bird watching point of view the site is known as an important observation point for migrants, both on land and sea. Being a natural promontory, Lavernock is excellent for studying visible coastal migration, with hundreds, sometimes thousands, of birds flying overhead or in the fields and hedgerows. In autumn, huge movements of Swallows, martins, Swifts, Skylarks, Meadow Pipits, Tree Pipits, Fieldfares, Redwings, Starlings and Chaffinches are regularly seen. Earlier in the season Yellow Wagtail and Pied/White Wagtail, Lesser Whitethroat and Wheatear are typical and Turtle Dove and Ring Ouzel have been noted. Late autumn can produce Firecrest, Brambling and Redpoll. Whinchats however are not as regular as they once were.

The point has a reputation for attracting rarities. Scarce species have included Eurasian Spoonbill, Honey Buzzard, Red Kite, Hoopoe, Wood Lark, Richard's Pipit, Common Nightingale, Icterine Warbler, Red-breasted Flycatcher, Red-backed Shrike, Great Grey Shrike, Snow, Lapland, Ortolan and Corn Bunting.

Lavernock is a prime sea-watching point. Viewing in stormy conditions from the cliff-top is not always easy. The pumping station on the cliff edge can afford some shelter. The old World War II lookout shelter has now been demolished but there is another overlooking St. Mary's Well Bay at the bottom end of the WTSWW reserve. Generally the observation of seabirds is best undertaken during spring and autumn migrations. The optimum conditions are during or just after south-westerly gales, when seabirds are driven up the Bristol Channel. The most regular species are Manx Shearwater, Fulmar, Gannet and Kittiwake. Occasionally small numbers of Common Scoter, Guillemot, Razorbill, Arctic and Pomarine Skuas and Storm-Petrel can be seen. Terns can pass in small numbers from April to late September. Divers are rather less frequent but do occur. A Long-tailed Skua, a Glamorgan rarity, visited this stretch of coast in September 1991.

Two walks are recommended. The first follows the coastal path, northwards towards Penarth, whilst the second goes through the WTSWW Reserve towards St. Mary's Well Bay.

For the former, walk from the car park, past the church (note the plaque on the wall that celebrates the fact that Marconi used the Point to transmit radio transmissions to Flat Holm in 1897) and on to the concrete path that leads left on to the coastal path, which has been upgraded recently. Take care, as the path runs quite close to the cliff edge in places. By following the path you will pass through a mixture of habitats. The cliff–top and field boundary hedgerows are berry-laden in autumn and can attract plenty of migrants. Redstart, Willow Warblers, Blackcap, Whitethroat and Chiffchaff are likely. In late autumn large flocks of Wood Pigeons may be seen. In winter, thrushes also use these hedgerows, stripping them of their fruit. Ivy-clad areas have attracted Firecrest in the past. The telegraph wires are good places to look for finches. Linnet, Goldfinch and Greenfinch are the most common. Hirundines tend to hunt across the fields, feeding up prior to setting off on their long migratory journey. It is also worth checking the fields. It depends on which crops have been sown as to the number and type of birds in the fields. If left to stubble, there can be good numbers of pipits and larks present. Kestrels and Peregrines regularly hunt the cliff-top fields and Ravens often pass overhead.

The second recommended walk is through the WTSWW Reserve towards St. Mary's Well Bay. From the car park, walk back up Fort Road for about 4–500 metres. En route, it is worth checking the fields and hedgerows on your right. Pass the caravan/chalet park on the left. The gate with an orange sign leads to the WTSWW reserve. This area consists of unimproved limestone grassland, with a rich flora, including Adder's-tongue Fern, a diminutive member of the fern family found in old pastures and similar long undisturbed habitats. Other plant species include Common Twayblade, Early Purple, Common Spotted, Greater Butterfly, Green-winged and Bee Orchids, Cowslip, Ragged Robin, Yellow-wort, Hemlock Water Dropwort, Glaucous Sedge, Pale Flax and Dyer's Greenweed. The whole area is also excellent for butterflies, especially in late summer when Red Admiral and Painted Lady can be present, along with Clouded Yellow, Common Blue, Small and Large Skipper and Small Copper.

Numerous grassy paths criss-cross the area and there are some stiles to negotiate. Check the isolated bushes in the meadow for Whitethroat and Lesser Whitethroat. The fields attract seed eaters in autumn. Breeding birds include most of the common passerines such as Wren, Dunnock, Blackbird, Greenfinch and Linnet. There is a small pond on the reserve edge where dragonflies are found in summer. The mix of species likely to be encountered are similar to those occurring on the cliff-top walk, however there are more woodland species here, including the occasional Spotted Flycatcher on migration. There are some old gun emplacements on the cliff-top. From here the path drops down to the bay. Here there is a shelter from which to sea-watch. The bay is a small tidal inlet which sometimes holds Oystercatcher, Curlew, Whimbrel and Turnstone. It is possible, with care, to carry on to Swanbridge and Sully Island.

Sully Island is only an island at high tide. Access can be gained by crossing the causeway opposite the Captain's Wife pub at low tide. It is best reached from the main road, taking the road on the left just before entering Sully. The island has a good range of small habitats: marine shore, coastal grassland, Gorse scrub with Bracken and bramble. It also has a small reed bed. Breeding species include Wren, Dunnock and Robin. Visitors include Rock Pipit, Stonechat, Kestrel, Greenfinch, Blackbird, Song Thrush and Carrion Crow. Migrants often use the island to rest. In winter, waders use the island as a high tide roost. There are records of Purple Sandpiper, Turnstone, Grey Plover, Ringed Plover, Knot, Oystercatcher and Curlew. More unusual records have included Turtle Dove, Green Woodpecker, Kingfisher and Water Rail.

Rock Pipit – Paul Parsons

51 – SOUTHERNDOWN

Southerndown (SS 8873) and Dunraven Park (SS 8972)

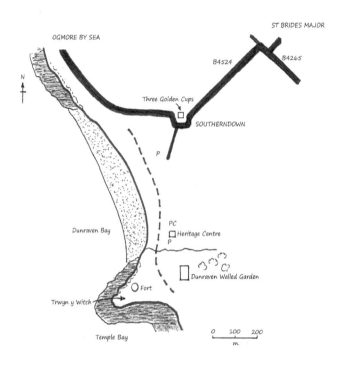

Access

Take the B4265 Southerndown road from either Ewenny or St. Brides Major, turn towards the sea at the 'Beach' sign, opposite the Three Golden Cups restaurant. Check for Little Owl in this vicinity. There are parking options at the top of the hill or by the beach. The former has a steep hill down to the beach, whilst the latter, for which a fee is payable, is near the Heritage Visitor Centre and shop. Sometimes, in the summer, the fields above the centre are used as an over-flow car park. There are toilets in this area. Wheelchair access is not particularly easy. The walk up to the walled garden is quite steep. The telephone number for the Glamorgan Heritage Coast Ranger Service is 01656 880157.

When to visit

Probably best at passage times and in the winter. It can get very busy in the summer months, as this is a very popular beach.

The site is owned by the Dunraven Estate. There is a walled garden and the remains of an Iron Age fort. Habitats include stony beach, rocky shoreline, cliffs, turf, scrub, mixed woodland and a seasonal stream. Plants include an array of limestone specialists such as Adder's Tongue and Maidenhair Ferns, Spurge Laurel, Stinking Hellebore, Wild Cabbage, Wild Madder, Purple Gromwell, Clustered Bellflower, Woolly and Tuberous Thistles as well as Green-winged Orchids. Over 30 butterfly species have been recorded.

The breeding list of the area is quite impressive with Buzzard, Kestrel, Peregrine, Tawny and Little Owl, woodpeckers, Herring Gull, Rock Pipit, Stonechat, Grasshopper Warbler and Spotted Flycatcher all recorded. The regionally scarce Grey Partridge and Barn Owl have bred in the locality. There is also a colony of cliff-nesting House Martins nearby.

Despite the long list of breeding birds, probably the best birding is in spring and autumn. Whimbrel and Wheatear can be seen on Trwyn y Witch in spring. The sheltered walled garden and adjacent scrub provide good bird watching opportunities, especially in autumn. Spotted Flycatchers and Common Redstarts regularly feed up here on return passage. A variety of warblers pass through and with luck, Pied Flycatcher and Firecrest too. Visible migration on autumn mornings can be impressive with large numbers of hirundines, wagtails, larks, pipits and finches (perhaps with attendant Merlin) possible, depending on conditions. An easterly wind generally produces the highest numbers. Snow Bunting has been recorded on the point. Dunraven is one of the best locations for Black Redstarts in Glamorgan. Search around the lodge and Visitor Centre in the winter months.

Also in winter, Red-throated Divers, Common Scoter, Kittiwake and Shag may be seen off-shore. Temple Bay can hold Curlew and Oystercatcher with the possibility of Purple Sandpiper on the rocks. Woodcock, Snipe and Water Rail can occur in the damp woodland. The hinterland is farmed organically and the stubbles can hold sizeable flocks of Linnet, Skylark and Stock Dove (a flock of 100 was seen in a recent winter). All the crow species can occur in this area, including Chough, that began colonisation in 1994. Numbers have increased and they can now be seen anywhere along the Heritage Coast.

52 – OGMORE
Ogmore River (SS 8776), Ogmore Estuary (SS 8575) and Ogmore-by-Sea (SS 8674)

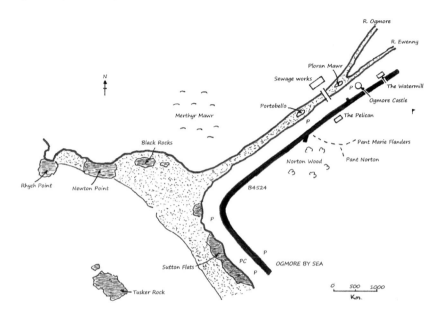

Access

Take the B4524 which follows the river down to Ogmore-by-Sea. For exploring the top of the estuary it is possible to park next to Ogmore Castle (SS 882769).
[Note that this car park can flood during spring tides],

Further downstream there are other parking options at Portobello (SS 874763) and Ogmore-by-Sea (SS 863756). There is a fee for parking at the last named. There are toilets at Ogmore-by-Sea. The sea-front footpaths are well maintained and wheelchairs can be used. Away from this area, access would be difficult.

When to visit

All year. Passage periods can be particularly rewarding. Hard winter weather can be productive at the Ogmore Estuary.

The Ogmore Estuary is a prime bird watching area. Most of the area is owned by the Merthyr Mawr and Dunraven Estates, yet there is de facto public access. The salt-marshes have been designated as an SSSI for their botanical value. Salt-marsh plants include Thrift, Sea-lavender, Sea Purslane, Scurvy-grass and the quite rare Sea-heath, which was discovered in 1981. Sea Beet and Sea Mayweed can be found on the pebble ridges. Another SSSI covers the rocks to the south of the river mouth because of their geological interest. There are a number of habitats - rocky shores, inter-tidal mudflats, dunes, flood meadows, Gorse hillsides through to mature woodland. There are two islands in the Ogmore River. The first is the grassy island of Ploran Mawr, which lies downstream of Ogmore Castle and close to a sewage works. A hundred metres downstream of the sewage works access bridge is the second island, Portobello, named after the nearby Portobello House. Hereafter the river becomes muddy and salt-marsh prevails

.

The Merthyr Mawr dunes form the northern boundary with Gorse and Bracken on either side. On the southern side, the mixed Norton Wood overlooks the river. The adjacent dry valleys of Pant Marie Flanders, Pant y Cwmteri and Pant Norton provide shelter for migrants. North of the river mouth is the extensive sandy beach at Newton, backed by the Merthyr Mawr dune system. The southern coast has rocky ledges called the Sutton Flats. All the sites suffer disturbance from visitors, dog walkers, joggers and horse riders. As a result early mornings are usually best for bird watching.

To cover the area thoroughly it is recommended that you work your way down the valley (or vice versa). Beginning at the Watermill, it is possible to pull in to the restaurant car park, which affords good views of the flood meadows. This area can hold large numbers of birds. Sometimes hundreds of gulls gather. Whilst Black-headed dominate, Mediterranean Gulls are frequent and a Laughing Gull dropped in during the 2005 national influx. Waders include Curlew, Lapwing, Oystercatcher, Redshank, Dunlin, Black-tailed Godwits etc. Grey Herons and Mute Swans are regular, as are Pheasant, Moorhen and various crow species. Little Egrets are being increasingly recorded, with up to seven together in recent winters. Green Sandpipers are regular in autumn and winter. Wood Sandpiper, an uncommon visitor to Glamorgan, has also occurred here. Red-necked Phalarope has been recorded twice, in November 2000 and October 2008. Wild geese are rare in the county (apart from Brent Geese in the far west). The Watermill has however hosted both Pink-footed and Bean Geese during severe cold spells. In autumn 2008 a

Whooper Swan spent a few weeks on the flood meadows, being the first to visit this site for several years.

Progressing down river, it is possible to overlook the islands of Ploran Mawr and Portobello. These islands provide refuges for both waders and gulls. When the tide is low, the exposed river banks can hold waders such as Common Sandpiper. This is probably the best spot in the county for observing Little Stint. In autumn they can arrive in good numbers (Glamorgan's highest tally was in September 1996, when 37 were observed). Amongst them in 1990 was a Semi-palmated Sandpiper. Another was found in 2001, these being the only two occurrences of this species in Glamorgan. Other passage waders that might be seen are Curlew Sandpiper, Ruff, Greenshank and Spotted Redshank. Grey Phalarope are occasionally recorded after autumn gales. Terns, although uncommon, have been seen at this site. The gardens of Portobello House are a magnet for migrant crests and warblers in autumn.

Red-necked Phalarope – Paul Parsons

In winter, duck numbers build up on the river. In addition to Mallard, good numbers of Little Grebe and Goldeneye can gather. The male Goldeneye are often seen performing their extravagant courtship display in late winter. Goosander and Shelduck are also regular, the latter often staying to breed in the dunes. Wigeon graze on the grass on the flood plain. Cold spells can result in an increase in duck numbers, with Smew and Scaup possible. On passage, Garganey has occurred, although they are uncommon. Rarities have included Great White Egret, White Stork , Spoonbill and Avocet.

Just inland from Portobello, on the Vale of Glamorgan side, are the dry valleys (or 'pants' in Welsh) that are worth investigating for passage passerines in late summer and autumn. Regulars include Spotted Flycatcher, Common Redstarts and common warblers. Both Turtle Doves and Dartford Warblers have been noted in the past. A real rarity, a Wryneck was found in Pant Norton in September 2008. The woods hold many common species. Both Pied Flycatcher and Wood Warbler have been seen on passage. Overhead the raptor species may include Buzzard, Peregrine and Kestrel. Goshawks have been seen but only rarely.

Goldfinches and Linnets tend to favour the salt-marsh and Pied Wagtails are relatively common here. On passage, Yellow and White Wagtails can also be seen. In most winters Water Pipits can be seen on the salt-marsh. Take care as *littoralis* race Rock Pipits have also been recorded. Both Peregrine and Merlin regularly hunt across this area. Passage Ospreys have been noted but never seem to linger. In winter, the scrub area bordering Merthyr Mawr can hold good numbers of Redwing and Fieldfare, feeding on the extensive yellow-berried Sea Buckthorn. Nearer the estuary, the Gorse bushes should be examined for Stonechat, Yellowhammer, Linnet, Dunnock, Wren and Dartford Warbler (outside the breeding season).

Gulls abound along the sea front. Common, Herring, Lesser and Great Black-backed are regular. Rarer gulls, such as Mediterranean, Little, Ring-billed, Glaucous, Iceland and Sabine's have occurred. Check the beach for Ringed Plover and the grassy areas for Oystercatcher. Cormorant seem to be ever present in the bay. Other sea birds are few but Red-throated Divers are possible in winter. From the far end of the car park a stile leads on to a grassy footpath. In winter, especially at high tide, Purple Sandpipers and Turnstones may be seen on the rocks.

On the short grass of the foreshore, Meadow and Rock Pipits are common. The 'special' bird of this area is undoubtedly the Chough. They are regularly seen feeding on the turf, often in the company of Jackdaws and Rooks. In recent winters a party of up to thirteen birds has been seen in this area. Wheatears also relish this habitat and one or two pairs may stay to breed. Scarcer visitors to Ogmore-by-Sea have included Black Redstart and Snow Bunting.

53 - NASH POINT (SS 9168)

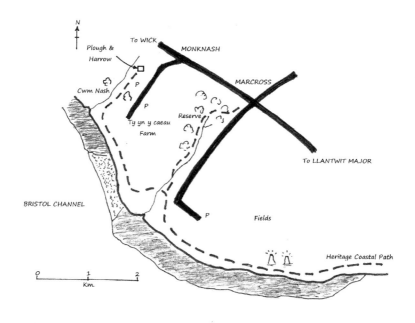

Access

This site, which is part of the Glamorgan Heritage Coast, lies about four kilometres west of Llantwit Major and is signposted off the B4265. The spectacular cliffs make this a particularly attractive area to visit. There is a large car park at the Point, for which a fee is payable. There are toilets near the car park and there are pubs in nearby Marcross and Monknash. Please note that the cliff edges are potentially dangerous. There is a well surfaced road leading from the car park to the lighthouses where wheelchairs could be used.

When to visit

Can be productive at any time of year but passage months are particularly recommended. Nash Point is probably at its best in autumn. The most interesting period is probably from mid August to the end of October. Early November can be rewarding, although the bulk of the migration is over by then. Nash Point is one of the best bird watching sites in the area as it has several diverse habitat types in a relatively small area. It is also an excellent migration watch-point.

From the car park there are two options: cliff-top walks to the east or exploration of the cliffs and cwms (valleys) to the north and west. For the former, walk along the cliff-top, past the lighthouses towards St Donats. On your left are a series of grazing fields. These grassy areas are good for pipits and wagtails. In autumn, check for Yellow Wagtails, especially if there is any stock in the fields, as they have the habit of 'following' grazing animals, feeding on insects disturbed by the grazers. Also at migration time Wheatear, Whinchat and Redstart may be found here. Around the lighthouses there are often pipits and wagtails strutting about on the closely grazed turf. With luck, a Black Redstart might be encountered around the lighthouses. Fulmars use the up-draughts from the cliffs to patrol the coast. In summer, look out for the colony of cliff-nesting House Martins. In the cliff-top scrub are Stonechat and commoner species such as Wren and Dunnock.

Wren – Bob Mitchell

From the lighthouses, cross the stone stile. Here are more arable many fields, some of which may be ploughed. They are well worth checking as they sometimes contain large numbers of birds, especially from August to November. In autumn, Skylarks, Meadow Pipits and Pied Wagtails are joined by Yellowhammers, Reed

Buntings, Chaffinches, Greenfinches and Goldfinches. Lapland and Snow Bunting have been recorded here in the past and Kestrel and Peregrine are both regular here. Choughs have recolonised this area and they may be encountered anywhere along the Heritage Coast from Nash Point to Ogmore. As is typical of a headland location, one would expect to observe overhead migration in autumn. Swifts move through in early to mid August. Early mornings in late August are the best time to see Tree Pipits, Redstarts and Wheatears, as they head south. In September, hirundines are perhaps the most visible migrants. They can occur in great numbers during the first three weeks of the month. With these may be the occasional Cuckoo or Turtle Dove. Keep an eye out for Hobbies during this period as they often follow the migrating Swallows and House Martins.

By continuing along the coastal path for about 1½ kilometres, one eventually reaches a wooded valley leading on to the Atlantic College site at St Donats. There is now the option of doubling back to Nash Point or heading inland on a circular walk via the lanes to Marcross, back to the starting point. In the hedgerows and farmland there should be Yellowhammer, Reed Bunting and Linnet. This is one of the few areas in the eastern part of Glamorgan where species such as Tree Sparrow and Grey Partridge can be found.

To the west lie the Marcross and Cwm Nash valleys. From Nash Point, the path drops quite steeply into a valley. At the foot of the slope, there are two options, head inland via the Marcross Valley or continue around the coast to Cwm Nash. The former funnels its way up the valley, almost as far as the village of Marcross. There is a rich variety of flora here. The area of Gorse and scrub at the entrance to the valley is particularly good for Linnets, Stonechats, Whitethroat and Lesser Whitethroat. It was here that a Barred Warbler was found in September 1994. The woodland area beyond has a footpath which runs right around the reserve. In spring and summer the sound of Willow Warblers, Chiffchaffs, Blackcaps and Garden Warblers appears to be everywhere. The wood is managed by the Coast Rangers and it now provides a more open and varied aspect, especially with the creation of small clearings. A Melodious Warbler was found in one of these glades in September 1993. Following the path out of the wood, towards the village, the churchyard is worth a look. It is particularly good for warblers, crests and flycatchers. Both Spotted and Pied Flycatchers have been recorded here.

Instead of following the Marcross Valley, there is an 8 kilometre circular route via Cwm Nash and Monknash. If you merely wish to walk the Cwm Nash Valley, there is a car park just below the Plough and Harrow pub, for which a fee is payable. By following the coastal path around the headland, you will eventually reach Monknash beach where the Heritage Coast Choughs are often encountered. From the beach, follow the footpath inland towards Monknash. This wooded valley can hold migrants in season. In the open areas to the south of Monknash you are likely to encounter a good selection of farmland species. Yellowhammer, Linnet, Tree Sparrow and Grey Partridge are all possible.

Sea-watching from the cliff-tops can be rewarding, especially from spring through to autumn. Look out for Gannet, Guillemot, Razorbill and occasionally wind-driven Manx Shearwaters and Storm-Petrels. Terns may be seen from May to September, with the most likely being Arctic and Common but Black and Little are no strangers. Sometimes skuas can be seen harrying the terns. Arctic Skuas are the most frequent although Great Skuas have been recorded and famously a Long–tailed Skua was seen in July 1992. In winter, Common Scoter are the most regular seaduck with Eider and Red Breasted Merganser also being possible. They may be seen from late summer onwards. Red Throated and Great Northern Divers have been recorded, although the latter is rare.

Other sites

It is impossible to cover every bird rich habitat in the county. There follows a list of some other sites that you might like to visit :

Bridgend
Ogmore Forest (SS 9489)
Tythegston (SS 8578)
Merthyr Mawr (SS 8777)

Cardiff
Flat Holm Island (ST 2265)
Howardian Nature Reserve (ST 2079)
Cefn Mably Woods (ST 2184)
Coed-y-Wenallt (ST 1583)

Neath-Port Talbot
Port Talbot Docks (SS 7689)
Gnoll Estate Country Park (SS 7697)

Swansea and Gower
Crymlyn Burrows (SS 7092)
Crymlyn Bog (SS 6994)
Fairwood Common (SS 5692)
Kilvrough Manor Woods (SS 5589)
Cefn Bryn (SS 4989)
Broad Pool (SS 4989 & 5191)
Pennard Burrows (SS 5488)
Loughor Bridge (SS 5697)

Caerphilly
Mynydd Eglwsilan (ST 1292)
Bargoed Country Park (ST 1599)
Gelligaer Common (ST 1398)

Merthyr Tydfil
Merthyr Common (SO 0710)
Cyfartha Park (SO 0307)

Rhondda Cynon Taff
Perthcelyn (ST 0597)
Craig-y-Llyn (ST 9003)
Hirwaun Pond (SN 9305)

The Vale of Glamorgan
Porthkerry Park (ST 0866)
Dyffryn Gardens (ST 0972)
Hensol Lake (ST 0478)
Ogmore Down (SS 8976)
River Ely (ST 0480 -- 0676)
Col-huw, Llantwit Major (SS 9567)
Castle upon Alun (SS 9074)

Species lists

Glamorgan species – where to find them
Table 1 : Glamorgan species
Table 2 : Rare birds recorded in Glamorgan

Goshawk with prey – Bob Mitchell

Glamorgan species – where to find them

This section is designed to help bird watchers who wish to see specific species. The 'Species' column of table 1 gives hints and tips on where in the county one might expect to see particular species. The 'Months/Status' column gives information on the most likely months in which to see the target species.

The current Glamorgan list is 328 species (as of April 2009). Some however are historic records, dating back to the 19th Century. Details on the very rare visitors can be found in table 2 on page 183.

Abbreviations used in the tables

AV	- Accidental visitor	Est.	- Estuary
IB	- Introduced breeder	Hd.	- Head
MB	- Migrant breeder	Fem.	- Female
NBR	- Non breeding resident	Fm.	- Farm
PM	- Passage migrant	Juv.	- Juvenile
RB	- Resident breeder	Pen.	- Peninsula
SV	- Summer visitor	Pt.	- Point
WV	- Winter visitor	Res.	- Reservoir

ENR   - Eglwys Nunydd Reservoir
CBWR- Cardiff Bay Wetlands Reserve
KNNR - Kenfig National Nature Reserve

The bird names in these tables are the British (English) vernacular names used in the BOU (British Ornithologists' Union) list. Resident breeders are assumed to be present in all months. Their numbers and their relative abundance in the year may vary with additional migrants, summer or winter visitors.

The numbers in brackets cross-reference the site guides. For example, Kenfig National Nature Reserve is described in site 1 – hence in the table it is designated - KNNR (1)

Table 1 : Glamorgan species

Species	Months Status
MUTE SWAN *Cygnus olor* Found on lakes throughout, especially at KNNR (1), The Knap, Ogmore Est. (52), Roath Park (20), Cosmeston (49) and CBWR (14).	RB
BEWICK'S SWAN *Cygnus columbianus* Rare vagrant, probably from Slimbridge WWT– Glos.	10-3 WV
WHOOPER SWAN *Cygnus Cygnus* Formerly a winter visitor to KNNR (1) but now quite uncommon. There were 2 at Ogmore Est. (52) in Nov. 2008.	10-3 WV
BEAN GOOSE *Anser fabilis* Rare	10-3 WV
PINK-FOOTED GOOSE *Anser brachyrhynchus* Rare	10-3 WV
WHITE-FRONTED GOOSE *Anser albifrons* Uncommon. Most occurrences are coastal in winter	10-3 WV
GREYLAG GOOSE *Anser anser* Feral flocks exist at Roath Park (20), Caerphilly Castle (7), Tirfounder Fields (35) and Oxwich (40). Truly wild birds are rare.	RB,IB
CANADA GOOSE *Branta canadensis* Seen on fresh water lakes and parkland, especially Margam Park (29), Tirfounder Fields (35), Parc Slip (3) and Caerphilly Castle (7).	RB,IB
BARNACLE GOOSE *Branta leucopsis* Rare	10-3 WV
BRENT GOOSE *Branta bernicla* Regular in the Burry Inlet (41) in winter. Most are 'dark bellied.' Flocks can reach several hundred. The less common 'pale bellied' also occurs on the south Gower coast e.g. Blackpill (39). Uncommon east of Swansea Bay.	10-3 WV
SHELDUCK *Tadoma tadoma* Several hundred may be found in the Burry Inlet (41) from Whiteford to Loughor. Frequently seen at Ogmore Est. (52). Formerly numerous in Cardiff Bay (before the impoundment of the bay) (14) They now tend to favour the Rhymney Est. (15). Occasionally at Aberthaw (48).	9-5 RB
MANDARIN DUCK *Aix galericulata* Irregular in occurrence, mostly around Cardiff. Most are probably escapees from collections. In the west, there have been regular occurrences at Margam Park (29), where breeding has taken place.	WV,IB
WIGEON *Anas enelope* Very numerous in the Burry Inlet (41) with over 1000 regularly wintering. Further east, uncommon but annual at Rhaslas/Butetown Ponds, KNNR (1), Ogmore Est. (52) and Aberthaw Quarry Pool (48).	9-4 WV
GADWALL *Anas strepera* Occur in winter at KNNR (1), with flocks of a dozen or more. In the west, may be found at ENR (28) and are increasingly being seen in the Burry Inlet/Loughor Est. (41).	8-5 WV

162

TEAL *Anas crecca* Most numerous on the north Gower saltings (42) and at Rhymney Est. (15) in the east. Relatively common on lakes with surrounding vegetation including CBWR (14), Tirfounder Fields, KNNR (1) and Parc Slip (3).	9-4 WV
MALLARD *Anas platyrhynchos* Very common on any river/lake. Hundreds may be present at Roath Park Lake (20) or the Glamorgan Canal. (22)	RB
PINTAIL *Anas acuta* Several thousand winter in the Burry Inlet. (41) Perhaps the best sites are Weobley and Llanrhidian. (42) In the east only found in numbers at the Rhymney Est. Very irregular elsewhere.	10-4 WV
GARGANEY *Anas querquedula* Uncommon short staying, passage migrant, particularly in spring, at ENR (28) and KNNR (1). Has occurred at Lamby Lake (16) recently.	3-4 PM
SHOVELER *Anas clypeata* Favoured localities in winter in the west are Llanrhidian, Wernffrwd (42) and ENR (28). Nowhere numerous but regular in small numbers in the east at KNNR (1), Ogmore Est./Watermill (52) and Llanishen/Lisvane Res. (19).	9-4 WV
RED-CRESTED POCHARD *Netta rufina* Uncommon: Most are thought to be escapees from wildfowl collections but sometimes found in autumn/winter, suggesting a more exotic origin.	AV
POCHARD *Aythya ferina* Difficult to miss at ENR (28), Llanishen/Lisvane Res., (19) Roath Park Lake (20), Cosmeston Lakes (49) and KNNR (1) in winter, when significant flocks arrive from the north. Some stay through the summer.	8-3 WV
RING-NECKED DUCK *Aythya collaris* Very rare American vagrant with only 8 records. The first was at Broad Pool, Gower in May 1989. Have occurred in both spring and autumn at KNNR (1), Cosmeston (49) and Llanishen/Lisvane Res. (19).	AV
FERRUGINOUS DUCK *Aythya nyroca* Very rare. Lisvane (19) has proved to be the 'hot spot' with 6 records. Have also been seen at Roath Park (20), ENR (28), Hensol and KNNR (1). The last was at Cosmeston (49) in Nov. 2008. Mainly occurs in Oct. and Nov.	10-11 AV
TUFTED DUCK *Aythya fuligula* Very common. They sometimes breed. Can be seen on any large lake in winter, with flocks often reaching 200.	RB
SCAUP *Aythya marilhea* Rather local in winter at Rhymney Est./Cardiff Bay (15/14) in small numbers. Occasionally at Burry Inlet (41), ENR (28), KNNR (1) and Cosmeston Lakes (49).	10-4 WV
EIDER *Somateria mollissima* Fairly common on Gower, where approximately 100 gather at Whiteford (41) in Feb. Regular on the south coast (e.g. Crabart (43) and elsewhere in the Burry Inlet. Uncommon in the east.	1-12 WV

LONG-TAILED DUCK *Clangula hyemalis* Now almost annual: Singles have been at ENR (28), Rhossili (43), KNNR (1), Llanishen/Lisvane Res. (19) latterly at Cardiff Bay (14) and Parc Cwm Darran (12).	10-2 WV
COMMON SCOTER *Melanitta nigra* This sea duck is seen off headlands on sea-watches, following stormy weather. They are very infrequent on inland waters. Hundreds can be seen off Rhossili in Nov./Dec. (43). Smaller numbers may be seen off the south Gower coast throughout the year.	4-11 WV
SURF SCOTER *Melanitta perspicillata* Only 6 records. ENR (28) has hosted two.	AV
VELVET SCOTER *Melanitta fusca* Uncommon but annual. May be seen in small numbers off the south Gower coast, late in the year.	WV
GOLDENEYE *Buchephala clangula* A winter visitor to areas such as Ogmore Est. (52) KNNR (1) and ENR (28). Can be seen displaying in early spring on the Ogmore.	11-4 WV,PM
SMEW *Mergellus albellus* Uncommon, typically occurring in hard winters on ice-free lakes, typically ENR (28) and KNNR (1). Very infrequent elsewhere.	12-3 WV
RED-BREASTED MERGANSER *Mergus serrator* Mainly coastal. Small numbers may be found around the north Gower coast in winter at Whiteford (41), Weobley, Llanrhidian (42) and Wernffrwd. Now quite scarce in eastern waters where sightings have generally been restricted to sea-watches after storms, at sites such as Breaksea Pt. (48).	10-3 WV
GOOSANDER *Mergus merganser* Quite common in the west, breeding on the Neath, Tawe and Loughor Rivers.. Increasing in the east, especially on the R. Taff, Cardiff Bay (14), Rhaslas Pond etc., Ogmore (52) and Parc Cwm Darran (12). In winter found on rivers and reservoirs.	RB
RUDDY DUCK *Oxyjura jamaicensis* Most frequently seen at ENR (28) and KNNR (1). Less frequent elsewhere.	10-5 AV
RED GROUSE *Lagopus lagopus* Uncommon and much sought after species in the county. A few exist in small areas of suitable heather moorland habitat north of Merthyr Tydfil.	RB
RED-LEGGED PARTRIDGE *Alectoris rufa* Rather uncommon. Usually found on farmland around Bridgend and the Vale of Glamorgan, where some have been released for sport shooting.	IB
GREY PARTRIDGE *Perdix perdix* Very local. May be found on the ash tips of Aberthaw power station - note that this is private property (48). Otherwise irregular on farmland sites along the coast, such as at Ty'n-y-Caeau Fm. in Marcross (53) and Slade Farm in Southerndown (51). Rare in the west but were formerly found at Whiteford (41).	RB

QUAIL *Cotumix cotumix* Almost a speciality of a single farm at Llanmaes but has been recorded more recently at Ty'n-y-Caeau (Marcross) (53), Sker fields (10), adjacent to the golf course and Llanilid. Believed to have bred recently.	4-8 PM
PHEASANT *Phasianus colchicus* Hard to miss around the Watermill and Ogmore Est. (52). Less regular but not uncommon elsewhere.	RB,IB
RED-THROATED DIVER *Gavia stellata* Regular in Swansea Bay (39). Also found along the south and south-west facing Gower coasts, especially Oxwich (40), Port Eynon (45) and Rhossili (43). Uncommon east of Port Talbot being restricted to coastal waters, lakes and docks. Most likely to be seen in winter on the sea at Porthcawl (2) Sker Pt. (1) or on inland lakes e.g. KNNR (1), Barry Docks, Cosmeston Lakes (49) and Llanishen/ Lisvane Res. (19).	9-4 WV
BLACK-THROATED DIVER *Gavia arctica* The rarest of the divers. Annual in Gower, with typically 3 or 4 in winter, where they may be seen from the headlands of the south coast or at Blackpill (39). In the east there have been only 32 records at sites such as Porthcawl (2), Cosmeston (49) and Llanishen Res. (19).	11-2 WV
GREAT NORTHERN DIVER *Gavia immer* Regular in Gower in the winter months and unlike the previous diver species often prefers to frequent the north Gower coast. Whiteford (41) is perhaps the most favoured location and recently Swansea's Queen's Dock has hosted one or two. Elsewhere they can be seen from the headlands. Scarce to the east of Port Talbot. Occasionally present in winter on lakes and docks e.g. ENR (28), KNNR (1) and Barry Docks.	4-5 11-1 WV
LITTLE GREBE *Tachybaptus ruficollis* Fairly common. Easy to see at Lisvane Res. (19) and Aberthaw (48). Present on many of the county's lakes.	RB,WV
GREAT CRESTED GREBE *Podiceps cristatus* Abundant, but local. Hard to miss at ENR (28), Margam Park (29), Cosmeston Lakes (49), KNNR (1), Hensol Lake and Cardiff Bay (14). Found in many other locations throughout the region.	RB,WV
RED-NECKED GREBE *Podiceps grisegena* Very uncommon. Has occurred at KNNR (1), Llanishen/Lisvane Res. (19) and Cardiff Bay (14). Rarely stay for more than a couple of days.	8-10 WV,PM
SLAVONIAN GREBE *Podiceps auritus* Scarce, but regular at favoured localities in Gower. Whiteford (41) hosts c.8 in winter. Less numerous elsewhere along the north Gower coast. Very infrequent winter visitor in the east, where historically KNNR (1) is the most favoured location.	11-1 WV,PM
BLACK-NECKED GREBE *Podiceps nigricollis* Rather scarce. As with Slavonian Grebe, they appear to prefer the north Gower coast and Whiteford (41) in particular, where they are strictly mid-winter birds. To the east, the bulk of records are from the last week of Aug. or first week of Sep. when passage migrants appear, especially at KNNR (1). Winter birds are scarce but occur from Nov. to Feb. and again KNNR (1)/ENR (28) are favoured locations.	8-9 11-2 WV,PM

FULMAR *Fulmarus glacialis* Breeds at numerous cliff sites on the south Gower coast with up to 70 being seen during coastal movements after storms. Further east, a few pairs breed on the cliffs from Nash Pt. (53) to Southerndown (51). May be seen from May to July from the point or along the coastal footpath. Irregularly seen in the Bristol Channel in all other months.	1-12 5-7 RB
CORY'S SHEARWATER *Calonectris diomedea* Very rare but could potentially be seen in late summer and autumn. Some influxes into the Bristol Channel have been quite large.	8-10 AV
SOOTY SHEARWATER *Puffinus griseus* Similar occurrence pattern to the other shearwaters. More likely to be seen during sea-watches at Port Eynon (45), where they could associate with Manx Shearwaters in late Aug.–early Sep. Very rare east of the Gower Pen. May possibly be seen off Porthcawl (2).	8-9 AV
MANX SHEARWATER *Puffinus puffinus* Quite abundant off the south Gower coast. Less often seen in the east. Frequently seen during sea-watches from Lavernock (50) and Sker Pt. (10). Counts of up to 3000 in a day have been reported from Porthcawl (2), almost exclusively in May.	4-9 SV,PM
BALEARIC SHEARWATER *Puffinus mauretanicus* Rare. Only really likely off Gower when they stray into the Bristol Channel. Tend to associate with Manx Shearwaters. In Aug. 2004 an exceptional flock of over 100 was seen off south Gower.	8-9 SV
STORM–PETREL *Hydrobates pelagicus* Storm-Petrels may breed on the coast of south Gower, where they are sometimes observed offshore in small numbers, especially at Mumbles Hd. (39). Quite scarce to the east of Gower. Appear in similar conditions that yield high numbers of Manx Shearwaters. In the breeding season there are infrequent sightings from the headlands at Nash (53), Porthcawl (2) and Sker (1).	4-10 RB?,SV
LEACH'S STORM–PETREL *Oceanodroma leucorhoa* Fewer occurrences than Storm Petrel but most likely in early winter (Oct./Nov.) following strong winds. Can seek safe haven on reservoirs. A huge 'wreck' occurred in Dec. 2006, with several inland records.	10-12 PM
GANNET *Morus bassanus* Regularly seen from coastal headlands during the summer months. In Gower, flocks rarely exceed 100. Much less numerous in the east.	4-10 SV
CORMORANT *Phalacrocorax carbo* Common and hard to miss at Whiteford (41), CBWR (14) and Roath Park (20) in particular. Also seen at all lakes and reservoirs and up the R. Taff to Aberdare and beyond.	NBR
SHAG *Phalacrocorax aristotelis* Fairly common resident west of Mumbles Hd. (39). Some breed at Worm's Hd. (43). Can be seen in small numbers off rocky coasts e.g. Crabart, Rhossili (43). Scarce in the east and strictly coastal (unlike Cormorant). Sometimes seen on sea-watches outside the breeding season with the Porthcawl area (2) giving the best opportunities. Singles are occasional seen in docks.	10-5 BR

BITTERN *Botaurus stellaris* Winter 'strongholds' are KNNR (1) and Cosmeston's West Lake (49) reed beds. where c. 5 birds may be present. Occasionally give superb flight views, especially at dawn or dusk.	11-3 WV
LITTLE EGRET *Egretta garzetta* Formerly rare but now colonising. Sites exist in both the east and west of Glamorgan. May be seen anywhere along the coast (inland records are few, but increasing). The best/most regularly visited sites are in the Loughor Est. (41) and along the north Gower coast. A roost of over 100 has been recorded below Woebley Castle (42). Generally less numerous in the east, however occurs regularly at KNNR (1), Ogmore Est., Aberthaw (48), CBWR (14) and Lamby Lake (16).	RB
GREY HERON *Ardea cinerea* Very common, regular and hard to miss. In the west, there are 11 heronries with about seventy nests. The east is not so well endowed. The highest numbers occur at the Hensol/Coed Llwyn Rhyddid and Ton Pentre heronries. Relatively high winter concentrations can occur at Tirfounder Fields–Aberdare (35). There is a new heronry near the ASDA store car park, adjacent to Forest Fm. (22).	RB
PURPLE HERON *Ardea purpurea* Extremely rare and only likely at substantial coastal reed bed sites, perhaps Oxwich (40), Crymlyn Bog, Cosmeston (49) and KNNR (1). There have been no recent records. Long awaited as a potential colonist	AV
WHITE STORK *Ciconia ciconia* Occasionally there are spring migrant 'overshoots'. Usually very brief visitors. Most sightings are coastal flight views.	5 AV
SPOONBILL *Platalea leucorodia* Whilst still rare, there have recently been annual occurrences on the Penclawdd salt-marsh, Gower (42).	AV
HONEY–BUZZARD *Pernis apivorus* Formerly rare, but now seen regularly in small numbers on passage,. Breed in the Vale of Neath at Afan Forest Park (30). They have occurred on passage at KNNR (1), Lavernock Pt. (50) and Rhossili (43) The RSPB may have telescopes set up in the car park in Resolven (31).	5-9 MB
RED KITE *Milvus milvus* Currently only regularly seen in the north of Glamorgan in the Gwaun-Cae-Gurwen area and the Taff Valley, north-west of Merthyr Tydfil. They may wander from further north, especially in the winter months. There is a southward expansion of breeding pairs in the county. Southern sightings are more likely to be in the first half of the year.	RB
MARSH HARRIER *Circus aeruginosus* Almost annual, yet scarce along the coast throughout, during migration. There have been just over 40 records in the county.	WV,PM
HEN HARRIER *Circus cyaneus* Our 'commonest' harrier although there are fewer than 20 reports each year. Seen in autumn/winter in both upland and lowland locations. A dusk visit to Llanrhidian (42) in Jan. is recommended.	10-4 WV

167

GOSHAWK *Accipiter gentilis* Increasingly reported and expanding its range. Though they may be reported from anywhere, they are most likely to be seen in the Afan Valley (30), Vale of Neath, Maesteg (5) Aberdare (34) and Llanwonno (33), where there are conifers.	RB
SPARROWHAWK *Accipiter nisus* The commonest small raptor. Most often reported from gardens. They are present throughout the year, though breeding reports are few.	RB
BUZZARD *Buteo buteo* Very conspicuous, universally common and hard to miss. Often seen on lampposts along major roads.	RB
OSPREY *Pandion haliaetus* Reported almost annually on north Gower, especially at Wernffrwd and Llanrhidian (42) in autumn. Erratic elsewhere, with fewer than five reports each year. Seems to prefer following river valleys as migration paths and coasting when reaching the sea in autumn.	4-5 9-10 PM
KESTREL *Falco tinnunculus* Once very common but now less so. Regular sightings come from Cardiff Gate, Rhymney Est. (15), Ogmore (52), Lamby Lake (16), CBWR (14) and the Garth (21). Fairly widespread in the west.	RB
MERLIN *Falco columbarius* Breeds in upland locations such as Parc Cwm Dare (34) and Garnwen (5) but the majority of reports are of winter birds. These come chiefly from coastal areas, especially north Gower, KNNR (1)/Sker/Ogmore (52) and Cardiff foreshore (15).	9-3 RB
HOBBY *Falco subbuteo* Uncommon migrant and possible breeder. There are around 30 reports a year, from many habitats especially lakes e.g. KNNR (1), Llanishen/Lisvane Res. (19).	4-10 RB?,SV
PEREGRINE FALCON *Falco peregrinus* Usually near sea cliffs and quarries. Up to 30 pairs breed annually. In winter usually seen near the coast. CCTV covers eyries at Dare Valley Country Park (34) and Cardiff City Hall (17).	RB
WATER RAIL *Rallus aquaticus* Secretive but rather noisy, when it's 'squeals' give it away. Patience can be rewarded at Cosmeston (49), KNNR (1) and the hides at Glamorgan Canal (22). Easier to see in the autumn and winter months.	RB,WV
MOORHEN *Gallinula chloropus* Very common on all inland waters – impossible to miss.	RB,WV
COOT *Fulica atra* Very common on freshwater pools and lakes.	RB,WV
CRANE *Grus grus* Rare with only 6 records (10 birds in total), the last was a group of 4 in 2005.	PM
OYSTERCATCHER *Haematopus ostralegus* Very common on Gower coasts, especially the Burry Inlet (41) and Blackpill (39). Locally common in the east. A resident flock frequents Southerndown (51) and Ogmore (52) beaches.	RB,WV

AVOCET *Recurvirostra avosetta* Uncommon and still only just over 40 records, despite national increases in breeding. There is a small breeding colony at Newport Wetlands, just to the east of the county.	SV
LITTLE RINGED PLOVER *Charadrius dubius* Has recently colonised the old Velindre works nr. Llangyfelach and Llanilid. Both these sites have uncertain futures. On passage can appear on the shoreline at KNNR (1) and Ogmore Est. (52).	4-9 RB,PM
RINGED PLOVER *Charadrius hiaticula* Common on sea shores throughout, particularly at Trecco Bay (2), Sker (1), Kenfig Beach (1) and Cardiff foreshore (15). Breeds at Whiteford (41) and Baglan. Forms flocks of up to 300 at Blackpill.	RB,WV
DOTTEREL *Charadrius morinellus* Probably occurs on passage each year but favours the lonely upland moors e.g. Mynydd Eglwysilan, where 'trips' have occurred in Apr.	4 PM
GOLDEN PLOVER *Pluvialis apricaria* Frequent the Burry Inlet (410 in winter, with several thousand birds being present e.g. Landimore and Crofty (42). Locally common in winter in the east. A large roving flock frequents the Sker (1) area. Breeding has recently been confirmed at an undisclosed site.	9-4 RB,WV
GREY PLOVER *Pluvialis squatarola* Seen in winter along the north Gower coast, especially at Weobley saltings (42). In the east, seen in small numbers in the first few months of the year at Rumney Great Wharf (15) and Sker Pt. (1).	1-3 PM,WV
LAPWING *Vanellus vanellus* More common in the north of the recording area, where it breeds on sparsely vegetated tips and other former industrial sites. Large flocks may form in cold weather movements, especially on the coast.	RB,WV
KNOT *Calidris canutus* Large numbers can be seen in winter at Whiteford (41) and Blackpill (39). Uncommon in the east. Most likely on Rumney Great Wharf (15).	8-3 PM,WV
SANDERLING *Calidris alba* Found on sandy shorelines. Present for much of the year at Blackpill (39) In the east, found on the beaches around Porthcawl (2), Kenfig Beach (1), Sker (1) and Ogmore (52) especially in Aug. and Sep.	7-5 PM,WV
LITTLE STINT *Calidris minuta* Uncommon but annual. Often seen associating with Dunlin at Blackpill (39) KNNR (1), Sker (1) and Ogmore Est. (52).	8-10 PM
PECTORAL SANDPIPER *Calidris melanotos* Rare with only ten records, all being from the KNNR (1) and Sker area. Only one record since 1988.	8 AV
CURLEW SANDPIPER *Calidris ferruginea* Autumn passage migrant in small numbers. Strictly coastal at Blackpill (39), Whiteford (41), Kenfig beach (1) Rumney Great Wharf (15).	8-9 PM
PURPLE SANDPIPER *Calidris maritime* Uncommon, however has been reported in winter from rocky shores such as Worm's Hd. (43), Mumbles Pier (39), Port Eynon Pt. (45), Port Talbot breakwater, Kenfig beach mussel beds (1) and Ogmore (52).	11-3 WV

DUNLIN *Calidris alpina* Large winter flocks can occur on the Gower Pen. at Blackpill (39) and in the east at Rhymney Est. (15) Less numerous elsewhere.	8-5 PM,WV
RUFF *Philomachus pugnax* Uncommon but reports are increasing, especially from the Gower coast, Sker/KNNR (1) and Ogmore (52) in winter.	8-2 PM,WV
JACK SNIPE *Lymnocryptes minimus* Most reports are from upland locations in winter. They often return to the previous year's haunts. In the west they are found at coastal sites e.g. Whiteford (41), Llanrhidian (42) and Baglan saltings.	10-3 WV
SNIPE *Gallinago gallinago* Widespread and fairly common winter visitor. May be found in any wet farmland in ditches etc. Currently the peak counts occur at Llanilid in Jan. Often seen from the KNNR (1) and Glamorgan Canal (22) hides and at CBWR (14). Sparse breeder in the uplands.	10-4 RB,WV
WOODCOCK *Scolopax rusticola* Probably breed in the Pelenna and Rheola forests and at Cwm Clydach (46). In the east, they-winter at Llanwonno (33) Best seen at dawn or dusk. In truth, they are probably more common than first thought.	9-5 RB,WV
BLACK-TAILED GODWIT *Limosa limosa* Uncommon. Now regularly seen at coastal locations and is likely at any time of the year. Most are seen in spring and autumn. Regular on north Gower (42) and Blackpill (39).	7-4 PM,WV
BAR-TAILED GODWIT *Limosa haemastica* Strictly coastal, mostly in winter/spring. Regularly seen at Whiteford, (41) Weobley (42) Blackpill (39) and Rhymney Est. (15).	1-5 PM,WV
WHIMBREL *Numenius phaeopus* Fairly common on passage, chiefly in Apr. and May e.g. North Gower, Swansea Bay (39), Rhymney Est. (15), Ogmore (52) and Sker (1). Less frequent in autumn.	4-5 8-11 PM
CURLEW *Numenius arquata* Common on coasts and present throughout the year. Some breed in the northern upland areas. Found in winter at the north Gower saltings (42) Rumney Great Wharf (15) and the Watermill, Ogmore (52).	RB,WV
COMMON SANDPIPER *Actitis hypoleucos* Chiefly a passage migrant that occasionally breeds. One has over-wintered in the Penclawdd Pill (42)recently. Passage birds may be seen at ENR (28), Llanishen/Lisvane Res. (19), Ogmore Est. (52) and KNNR (1). Can be found on upland streams in the breeding season.	4-9 MB,PM
GREEN SANDPIPER *Tringa ochropus* Present in most months of the year along the River Ely from the M4 motorway south to Peterston-super-Ely. Has wintered at the Watermill (52). Elsewhere, a passage migrant to the north Gower coast, typically in the second half of the year.	7-12 PM,WV
SPOTTED REDSHANK *Tringa erythropus* Uncommon but regular in the west at Whiteford (41) and Blackpill (39). Rare in the east. One was at Ogmore Est. (52) in the winters of 2005 and 2006.	9-10 PM,WV

GREENSHANK *Tringa nebularia* Regularly winters in small numbers in the Burry Inlet (41). Not numerous anywhere. Most likely on autumn passage as a visitor to lakes and shores, typically singly or in small groups.	4-9 PM,WV
WOOD SANDPIPER *Tringa glareola* Very uncommon visitor in autumn to lakes and reservoirs e.g. Llanilid, Llanishen/Lisvane Res. (19) and KNNR (1). Rare in west.	8 PM
REDSHANK *Tringa tetanus* Fairly common in Gower but in the east is only numerous at the Rhymney Est. (15) where several hundred can be present throughout the year. The flock of c.500 at the Taff/Ely Est. apparently died out or dispersed after the Cardiff barrage was built.	RB,WV
TURNSTONE *Arenaria interpres* Relatively common on rocky coasts. Found in the east at Sker, Porthcawl seafront, Rest Bay rocks (2) and Cardiff foreshore (15).	NBR
RED-NECKED PHALAROPE *Phalaropus lobatus* Rare. The last two have both been at the Watermill flood (52) in 2000 and 2008, comprising the ninth and tenth county records.	11 PM
GREY PHALAROPE *Phalaropus fulicarurius* Only likely after stormy weather in autumn. Recent records include birds at ENR (28), R. Ogmore (52) and Lamby Lake (16).	9-10 PM
POMARINE SKUA *Stercorarius pomarinus* Uncommon and only likely to be seen during sea-watches in spring and autumn. There have been over 50 records, mostly off south Gower headlands. Can be seen in very small numbers in May.	4 8-10 PM
ARCTIC SKUA *Stercorarius parasiticus* Uncommon passage migrant, seen in spring during sea-watches. Annual from Aug. to Nov. off the south Gower headlands. Can be seen irregularly from Cardiff foreshore (15).	4-10 PM
LONG-TAILED SKUA *Stercorarius longicaudus* Rare. There have been 9 records, with only one since 1992.	PM
GREAT SKUA *Stercorarius skua* Uncommon. May be seen on sea-watches, especially from the south Gower headlands and Porthcawl (2), Nash (53) and Lavernock Pt. (50) in the east.	PM
SABINE'S GULL *Xema sabini* Very uncommon. After storms, frequents lakes rather than shores. Recorded offshore at Porthcawl (2) and Blackpill (39) during sea-watches.	AV
KITTIWAKE *Rissa tridactyla* Breeds at Mumbles Pier (39). Often seen from the coastal headlands, when conditions are right. Dozens can be seen on sea-watches, when breeding birds from the west are driven up channel by storm conditions. Rare in the winter months.	3-10 RB
BONAPARTE'S GULL *Chroicocephalus philadelphia* Rare. There have been only 6 records - with Cardiff Bay (14) recording half of the county records. They usually associate with Black-headed Gulls.	3-4 AV

BLACK-HEADED GULL *Chroicocephalus ridibundus* Common throughout..	NBR
LITTLE GULL *Hydrocoloeus minutus* Regularly seen on passage at Cardiff Bay (14) and off Aberthaw (48), either singly or in small numbers and occasionally at KNNR (1) and ENR (28). In the west, they have been known to over-winter but are mostly frequently seen from Port Eynon (45) and the coastal stretch from Port Talbot to Mumbles (39) on passage.	8-3 PM,WV
MEDITERRANEAN GULL *Larus melanocephalus* Formerly rare but now regular along the coast, especially at Blackpill and Bracelet Bay (39). They can be seen there in most months. Less likely to be seen from Apr. to Jul. In the east, Porthcawl sea front (2), Ogmore Est. (52) and Cardiff Bay (14) are perhaps the most frequented sites.	PM,WV
COMMON GULL *Larus canus* Common in winter at Blackpill (39) and Whiteford (41), sometimes reaching four figures. In the east, small numbers occur in winter, along the coast and adjacent lakes. Not as numerous as in the past.	10-3 PM,WV
RING-BILLED GULL *Larus delawarensis* Rare. Seen almost annually at coastal locations e.g. Rhymney Est., (15) Lamby Lake (16) , Cosmeston (49), Porthcawl (2) Sker (1), Cardiff Bay (14) and Blackpill (39), chiefly in winter. The first British record was from Blackpill in Apr. 1973.	AV
LESSER BLACK-BACKED GULL *Larus fuscus* Common and widespread, especially in the Cardiff area, where pairs breed on factory roofs. Flat Holm has a breeding population of several thousand pairs.	RB
HERRING GULL *Larus argentatus* Common, but not as numerous as in the past. Flat Holm has c. 400 breeding pairs. Others breed along the Heritage Coast. Can reach several thousand around the Lamby Way tip (15).	RB
YELLOW-LEGGED GULL *Larus michahellis* Uncommon. In the west they have occurred quite regularly within flocks of other gulls, apparently preferring the mud flats of the north Gower coastal strip. Uncommon in the east and largely absent in the summer months. Most reports emanate from the south-east coastal area.	1-4 8-12 AV
ICELAND GULL *Larus glaucoides* Formerly annual. Most often seen in spring at locations such as Cardiff foreshore (15), Cosmeston Lakes (49) and Ogmore Est. (52).	3-4 AV
GLAUCOUS GULL *Larus hyperboreus* Almost a reversal in occurrence with Iceland Gull. Seen in winter and spring with around 40 records. Now almost annual.. Favoured spots are Lamby Way tip (15) in the east and Swansea Bay (39) in the west.	11-4 AV
GREAT BLACK-BACKED GULL *Larus marinus* Common resident but rarely numerous. Numbers may reach c.100 at Blackpill and 50 at Rhymney Est. (15) in winter. Though typically coastal, they can occur on inland lakes.	RB

BLACK TERN *Chilidonias niger* Regularly seen on migration in spring and more frequently in autumn at KNNR (1) and ENR (28). Less frequently seen off-shore from Mumbles (39) east to Salthouse Pt. (42).	5-9 PM
WHITE-WINGED BLACK TERN *Chilidonias leucopterus* Rare with fewer than 10 records. Often associate with Black Tern on migration and favour lakes e.g. KNNR (1).	PM
SANDWICH TERN *Sterna sandvicensis* Annual on sea-watches from Apr. to Sep. Sometimes seen in small groups, particularly off Port Eynon (45) on the south Gower coast, In the east, Porthcawl (2) and Sker (1) are favoured. Rare inland.	3-10 PM
COMMON TERN *Sterna hirundo* Seen on passage, both on the coast and on inland lakes and reservoirs e.g. Gower from Blackpill (39) to Loughor (41). Less frequent but regular at Cardiff Bay (14) and Llanishen/Lisvane Res. (19).	4-9 PM
ROSEATE TERN *Sterna dougallii* Rare. There have been fewer than 20 records.	AV
ARCTIC TERN *Sterna paradisaea* Uncommon and possibly decreasing. Likely in small groups on their spring migration along the channel coast.	4 PM
GUILLEMOT *Uria aalge* Relatively common. Formerly bred at Worm's Hd. (43) but possibly lost as a breeding species. Also seen at locations on the south Gower coast during the breeding season. Uncommon but fairly regular from sea-watches in the east of the county, notably around Porthcawl (2).	3-10 RB?
RAZORBILL *Alca torda* Less common than Guillemot but follows the same pattern of occurrence. Formerly bred at Worm's Hd. (43) and like the Guillemot may no longer do so. Occasional visitor to the Burry Inlet (41). Rare up-channel.	RB?
LITTLE AUK *Alle alle* Most likely to be seen when 'wrecked' following a storm. Very rarely seen at sea. There have been c.40 records.	PM
PUFFIN *Fratercula arctica* Very scarce off Worm's Hd. (43). Very rare in the east.	SV
ROCK DOVE/FERAL PIGEON *Columbia livia* Mostly feral. Generally found in towns and cities. Some may be found on rocky cliffs on the Heritage Coast (53) and Gower.	RB
STOCK DOVE *Columba oenas* Quite common on lowland farms. Can form large winter foraging flocks e.g. Southerndown (51) and Cwm Nash (53).	RB
WOOD PIGEON *Columba palumbus* Very common throughout. Huge migrating and wintering flocks can occur, especially on the coastal fringe e.g. Vale of Glamorgan (53).	RB
COLLARED DOVE *Streptopelia decaocto* Common throughout, with a preference for human habitation, particularly preferring to nest in Leylandii trees. There has been evidence of a slight decrease in numbers recently.	RB

TURTLE DOVE *Streptopelia turtur* Uncommon but singles do occur annually. On migration they may be seen anywhere in the lower half of the county, typically in early Jun.	5-6 SV
CUCKOO *Cuculus canorus* Formerly common in the upland areas of the west though appears to be in decline. Was once common in the reed beds of KNNR (1) and Oxwich (52) but has declined here too. Now confined to uplands areas such as the Lynfi Valley (6), Rudry Common (9) and the Garth (21).	4-8 RB
BARN OWL *Tyto alba* Uncommon, although numbers appears to be recovering. The main distribution is in the Llynfi Valley (6) and upland areas. Winter dispersal brings them to lower altitudes. In the west, they are a scarce resident, often seen in winter at Llanrhidian (42).	RB
LITTLE OWL *Athena noctua* Less common than it was. Fairly regular at Wentloog Level/Mardy Fm.(150 in the east and Sker Fm. (1) in the west. There are several pairs in the Lynfi Valley (6). In the far west they frequent river valleys and upland areas but are not common anywhere.	IB
TAWNY OWL *Strix aluco* Fairly common in woodland throughout. Usually located by their distinctive calls in early spring and autumn. Frequent in towns and cities. The Cardiff parks e.g. Heath Park, Roath Park, Bute Park (17) and Forest Fm. (22) usually have pairs. Common also in upland areas. The Llynfi Valley (6) has many breeding pairs.	RB
LONG-EARED OWL *Asio otus* Uncommon and local. Probably under-recorded, especially in upland areas. They often appear in winter and tend to have some roosting site fidelity e.g. Kenfig dunes (1) and Wentloog levels (15) occasionally.	WV
SHORT-EARED OWL *Asio flammeus* Uncommon winter visitor. Seen on Margam Moors (28) Llanrhidian Marsh (42) Kenfig (1), Wentloog (15) and more recently, Llanilid.	10-5 WV
NIGHTJAR *Caprimulgus europaeus* Utilises the clearings in conifer forests. Breeding numbers are increasing. Regularly breeds at Pen Disgwylfa, Ogmore Forest, Llanwonno (33) and Garnwen (5)	5-7 MB
SWIFT *Apus apus* Common, especially in the valleys, where they breed in roof spaces. In times of low cloud and on passage can occur in large concentrations at larger lakes and reservoirs e.g. ENR (28), KNNR (1) and Cardiff Bay (14).	5-9 MB
ALPINE SWIFT *Apus melba* Rare with fewer than 10 records. There may be chance of one in early Swift migrations in May. Their larger size and white under parts are particularly noticeable. Typically brief visitors.	AV
KINGFISHER *Alcedo atthis* Present on most local rivers and lakes. Hard to miss from at Forest Fm. (22). They are even in Cardiff along Taff from the Millennium Stadium to the Bay (14). Generally less common in the west.	RB

BEE-EATER *Merops apiaster* There have been three reports involving 9 birds. Visits are typically brief. The first was at St. Athan on 6th July 1965.	6-10 AV
HOOPOE *Upupa epops* Rare but they are almost annual with c. 50 records. They favour gardens and secluded farmland localities on the coast.	AV
WRYNECK *Jinx torquilla* Rare. Usually seen in autumn. Passage migrants have occurred at KNNR (1), Llanwonno (33), Rudry Mountain (9), Aberthaw (48), Llangynwyd (6), Cosmeston (49) and the Ogmore 'Pants'(52).	9-10 PM
GREEN WOODPECKER *Picus viridis* Common and increasing in pastures, gardens and woodlands. Most often being located by their laughing/yaffling call.	RB
GREAT SPOTTED WOODPECKER *Dendrocopos major* Common in most deciduous woods/parkland. In the west they are found particularly in Cwm Clydach (46) and Clyne Woods (39). In the east at Bute Park (17), Coed y Bedw (21), Roath Park (20) etc.	RB
LESSER SPOTTED WOODPECKER *Dendrocopos minor* Rare and very erratic. Most often noted when calling in the breeding season, before the canopy develops. In the west, try Caswell Valley/Bishop's Wood or Clyne Valley (39). In the east they have been seen in Bute Park (17), Bryngarw CP (4) Miskin, Forest Fm. (22) and Lisvane (19).	RB
WOODLARK *Lullula arborea* Rare but now annual at migration points such as Lavernock Pt. (50) and Mewslade (44). Also a winter vagrant to KNNR (1) and Llanilid.	10-12 AV
SKYLARK *Alauda arvensis* Common, though declining. Found especially on the hilltops. Fairly large groups may occur in winter in the Vale of Glamorgan e.g. c.300 around Nash (53) and Marcross. Easily located at Whiteford. (41).	RB
SAND MARTIN *Riparia riparia* Usually the earliest hirundine to arrive. They can occur in large numbers, hunting insects over lakes such as Cardiff Bay (14). Numbers appear to be recovering. As breeding commences they tend to become more localised. At Junction 34 of the M4 there is a thriving breeding colony on the adjacent River Ely. Colonies also exist at Forest Fm. (22), Caerphilly Castle moat (7) and Bridgend town centre.	3-9 MB
SWALLOW *Hirundo rustica* Common, particularly in rural areas. Breeds in barns and out-buildings. Can be observed near large water bodies. Huge numbers can migrate south over Lavernock Pt. (50) in Oct.	4-10 MB
HOUSE MARTIN *Delichon urbicum* Common and numerous locally during the breeding season, when they congregate in colonies of mud nests glued to the eaves of dwellings. Cliff-nesting colonies exist on the Heritage Coast (53).	4-10 MB
RICHARD'S PIPIT *Anthus richardi* Rare with fewer than 13 records to date. Recorded on autumn migration at watch points. One over-wintered at Llanilid in 2003/4.	9-10 AV

TREE PIPIT *Anthus trivialis* Locally common breeding species and passage migrant in upland hills and moors with scattered trees e.g. Caerphilly ridge (11). Breeds only sparingly south of the M4 motorway. The Llynfi Valley (6) is a stronghold. On autumn migration can be seen from coastal watch points such as Lavernock Pt. (50).	4-9 MB
MEADOW PIPIT *Anthus pratensis* Common and occasionally numerous throughout. Can be encountered in mountainous areas as well as coastal habitats such as the fields on the Ogmore coast (52).	RB
ROCK PIPIT *Anthus petrosus* Common on all rocky seashores. As with Meadow Pipit, they can be seen along the shoreline at Ogmore (52) and even at Cardiff Bay (14).	RB
WATER PIPIT *Anthus spinoletta* The only regular locations are Portobello Island in the Ogmore River (52) and the slipway on Llwyn-on Res. (25) in winter.	11-2 PM,WV
YELLOW WAGTAIL *Motacilla flava* Irregular and erratic breeder. Seen on spring and especially autumn migration on the coast, where they often follow livestock. Annual in May and Aug. at ENR (28) and Rumney Great Wharf (15).	4-9 MV,PM
GREY WAGTAIL *Motacilla cinerea* Common on rivers and streams throughout, especially in the uplands.	RB
PIED WAGTAIL *Motacilla alba* Common. There are large roosts in town centres on tree lined busy streets and factory roofs. Often seen foraging in open areas such as supermarket car parks. Migrant 'White' Wagtails are scarce but regular on coasts at migration times.	RB
WAXWING *Bombycilla garrulous* Winter 2004/5 saw an unprecedented invasion of several hundred birds, prior to this only a handful had ever been recorded.	AV
DIPPER *Cinclus cinclus* Cleaner rivers have aided the spread of Dippers. They breed along the many rivers in the region e.g. Rivers Neath, Ely, Taff and many others.	RB
WREN *Troglodytes troglodytes* Common in woodlands and gardens throughout.	RB
DUNNOCK *Prunella modularis* Common in open bushy country and gardens throughout.	RB
ROBIN *Erithacus rubecula* Common garden and woodland bird throughout. However many of our 'winter' Robins are actually migrants from continental Europe.	RB
NIGHTINGALE *Luscinia megarhynchos* Rare. The most recent sightings have been singing males in spring at Llanedeyrn and on the Caerphilly ridge (11).	AV
BLACK REDSTART *Phoenicurus ochruros* Uncommon but regular winter visitor to places such as Aberthaw Power Station/Gileston (48) in winter. Has recently been seen on the Cardiff Bay barrage (14). On Gower can be seen in autumn/winter on rocky coasts such as Cwm Ivy (41).	PM,WV

REDSTART *Phoenicurus phoenicurus* Prefers open Oak woodland, such as that found on the Garth and Coed-y-Bedw (21). Generally more numerous in the north at Hirwaun, Pontneddfechan (32) and Penderyn (26). Absent as a breeding species on Gower but does breed in the western uplands of the county.	4-9 MB
WHINCHAT *Saxicola rubetra* Declining in numbers and now localised. Can be seen on spring and autumn passage near the coast, where they may occur in arable fields. Breeds in uplands e.g. Llynfi valley (6) , Cilfynydd and Aberdare (34).	4-10 MB
STONECHAT *Saxicola torquatus* Resident. Increasing, possibly at the expense of the Whinchat. Favours Gorse and un-maintained land, shunning urban and agricultural areas. e.g. KNNR (1), where it is the Reserve symbol.	RB
WHEATEAR *Oenanthe oenanthe* Breeds predominantly in the hills on or adjacent to rocky outcrops and scree slopes. Cefn Sychbant/Cwm Cadlan (26) is a favoured location. Small numbers breed on the coast. On migration, they are commonly seen at coastal locations e.g. Sker (1) and Ogmore (52).	3-10 MB
RING OUZEL *Turdus torquatus* May be encountered in the uplands in the north of the county. Formerly bred but is in rapid decline. Exceptionally the autumn of 2005 produced record numbers of passage migrants in the east. Best located in Oct. at sites such as Parc Cwm Dare (34) or Cefn Sychbant (26).	3-11 MB,PM
BLACKBIRD *Turdus merula* Common throughout. As with Robins, their numbers are swelled by continental migrants in winter.	RB
FIELDFARE *Turdus pilaris* Common, yet localised. In winter, flocks may number several hundred descending on berry-bearing bushes. This behaviour is witnessed each year at Candleston, where birds feed on the orange Sea Buckthorn berries. Also at Ogmore and Merthyr Mawr (52)	10-3 WV
SONG THRUSH *Turdus philomelos* Fairly shy and retiring, preferring parkland and woodland with good cover. Repetitive song can be heard in spring. Generally easy to see in urban parks such as Bute Park around the Pontcanna horse paddocks (17), Forest Fm. (22) and Singleton Park in Swansea. Fairly numerous in the upland areas.	RB
REDWING *Turdus iliacus* Found in similar habitats to Fieldfare but more numerous, with typically heavy passage during autumn migration. .	8-4 WV
MISTLE THRUSH *Turdus viscivorus* Widespread resident breeding thrush that prefers woodland (especially Oaks) and farmland habitat. Often seen in highly vocal post-breeding family parties of c. 7 individuals.	RB
CETTI'S WARBLER *Cettia cetti* The range of this species appears to be expanding. They now breed at Oxwich (40) , Crymlyn Bog, Tennant Canal, ENR (28), Pant y Sais Fen and KNNR (1).	RB

GRASSHOPPER WARBLER *Locustella naevia* The best time and place to see these birds is at KNNR (1) or ENR (28), in mid Apr., when migrants appear and the 'reeling' sound of the singing males reveals their location. Elsewhere they are rather erratic in occurrence. They may breed anywhere that there is suitable habitat e.g. Oxwich (40) and Pant y Sais Fen etc.	4-9 MB
AQUATIC WARBLER *Acrocephalus paludicola* All records have been from KNNR (1) with most being caught during mid Aug. ringing sessions.	8 AV
SEDGE WARBLER *Acrocephalus schoenobaenus* Fairly common warbler in the scrub adjacent to lakes and reed beds throughout, especially ENR (28).	4-10 MB
REED WARBLER *Acrocephalus scirpaceus* Fairly common warbler, breeding in reed beds throughout e.g. ENR (28), Oxwich (40), Pant y Sais Fen, Crymlyn Bog, KNNR (1), Forest Fm., (22) Nelson Bog (13) etc.	4-10 MB
BLACKCAP *Sylvia atricapilla* Common breeding woodland warbler e.g. Glamorgan Canal (22). May also over-winter, when they are regular visitors to garden feeding stations. Wintering birds are thought to be from the continent.	1-12 MB
GARDEN WARBLER *Sylvia borin* Rather local in distribution. Breeding occurs in their preferred undisturbed, bushy woodland habitat. Can be quite secretive but easily located by their distinctive call. Coastal on migration.	4-9 MB
LESSER WHITETHROAT *Sylvia curruca* Though less common than Whitethroat, they occupy similar habitat and are quite vocal in early spring. May be found in bushy habitat throughout e.g. KNNR (1) and Aberthaw (48).	4-9 MB
WHITETHROAT *Sylvia communis* Relatively common but rather localised. Prefers rural, bushy locations e.g. ENR (28), KNNR (1), Cefn Bryn and Worm's Hd. (43).	4-10 MB
DARTFORD WARBLER *Sylvia undata* Benefiting from warmer winters. Breeds in Gorse habitat. Rhossili (43), Pennard and Ogmore (52) are favoured, although pairs have been seen in the Llynfi Valley (6).	RB
YELLOW - BROWED WARBLER *Phylloscopus inornatus* Rare (less than 20 records) but now almost annual. Usually seen in Oct and Nov. In the west, Mewslade and Cwm Ivy (41) are good places to search for them and in the east, Nantyfyllon (6) appears to be a 'hot spot' to rival KNNR (1), 2005 and 2008 were big years for this species.	10-11 AV
WOOD WARBLER *Phylloscopus sibilatrix* Uncommon. On passage usually seen in spring at woodlands such as the Wenallt (23) and Coed-y-Bedw (21), where their distinctive song enables them to be located. More commonly encountered in upland woods such as the Llynfi Valley (6) and Pontneddfechan (32).	5-7 MB
CHIFFCHAFF *Phylloscopus collybita* Common. They pass through KNNR (1) in numbers in spring. Many over-winter. 'Eastern' race birds have occurred at KNNR (1) in winter.	1-12 MB

WILLOW WARBLER *Phylloscopus trochilius* Common, especially at KNNR (1) in spring and summer.	3-10 MB
GOLDCREST *Regulus regulus* Common. They prefer old yew trees and pines and are generally faithful to these locations. e.g. Bute Park (17) , Cardiff and the Whiteford pine belt (41). Numbers can be swelled with continental migrants.	RB
FIRECREST *Regulus ignicapilla* Usually has the status of winter resident (with typically 5-10 present in the west) and passage migrant that might potentially breed. Erratic in occurrence but may associate with tit flocks in winter, as does Goldcrest. Recently one or two have over-wintered in Bute Park. (17) Otherwise try the same locations as Goldcrest.	10-3 PM,WV
SPOTTED FLYCATCHER *Muscicapa stiata* Breeds fairly widely, showing some site fidelity, however they are nevr really common anywhere. Known to breed around the Miskin Manor Hotel and Bryngarw CP (4). They are more common in the west, breed at Felindre, River, Dulais, Rheola Forest, Margam Abbey (29) and Pontrhydyfen.	5-9 MB
PIED FLYCATCHER *Ficedula hypoleucha* Localised breeding populations are present at nest box schemes e.g. Cwm Clydach (46). The species appears to be in decline. Some may occur at migration points e.g. Lavernock Pt. (50), Cwm Nash (53) etc.	4-9 MB
BEARDED TIT *Panurus biarmicus* Very uncommon/rare visitor to reed beds e.g. KNNR (1). The most recent were in CBWR (14) in Mar. 2007 and Cosmeston Lakes (49) in Nov./Dec. 2008. Potential colonist.	10-11 AV
LONG-TAILED TIT *Aegithalos caudatus* Common throughout, usually in parties of c. 12 and possibly as members of larger roving tit flocks in winter. Hard to miss.	RB
BLUE TIT *Cyanistes caruleus* Very common and widespread in gardens and woodland. Readily use garden nest boxes.	RB
GREAT TIT *Parus major* Common though less numerous than Blue Tit.	RB
COAL TIT *Periparus ater* Common, especially in coniferous and mixed woodland areas. Frequent visitor to garden feeding stations. Generally they are more numerous in the north of the county.	RB
WILLOW TIT *Poecile montana* Declining. Most reports come from upland areas of the county, with regular haunts in the Cynon Valley area e.g. Tirfounder fields. (35) and Pwll Gwaun Cynon (36). Very localised in the west.	RB
MARSH TIT *Poecile palustris* Most regular in the west at the Clyne Woods (39) and Cwm Clydach (46) breeding sites. Decreasing in the east and now rather irregular and hard to find. Most reports are from the Craig-yr-Allt ridge. (23) Reports generally relate to birds visiting garden feeders in winter.	RB

NUTHATCH *Sitta europaea* Usually found in similar habitat to Treecreeper. Seem to be on the increase. Hard to miss at the Glamorgan Canal/Forest Fm. feeding stations (22), where they may be extremely tame and bold, especially in winter. Their fluty calls are a key indicator of their presence, especially in summer.	RB
TREECREEPER *Certhia familiaris* Common though often hard to locate. Many breed in the Llynfi Valley (6). Frequently encountered at Bryngarw CP (4), Forest Fm. (22), Roath Park (20) and Hensol .	RB
GOLDEN ORIOLE *Oriolus oriolus* Rare. There have been only 16 records. The last being at Llanrhidian (42) in May 2008.	AV
RED - BACKED SHRIKE *Lanius collurio* Rare, there have been just 13 records since 1950. The last was on the west Gower coast at Broughton Bay in 2005.	AV
GREAT GREY SHRIKE *Lanius ecubitor* Rare with only 20 records. Prefer clear felled forestry plantations in winter e.g. Mynydd Margam (29) and Llanwonno (33).	WV
WOODCHAT SHRIKE *Lanius senator* Rare with only 8 records. The last two being at Cosmeston (49) in May 2002 and Rhosilli Down (43) in June 2009.	AV
JAY *Garrulus glandarius* Common, though more secretive than Magpies, for example. They appear to prefer wooded parkland habitat e.g. Hensol, Bute Park, (17) Forest Fm. (22) Most obvious on autumn migration, when they can occur in fairly large flocks. Resident birds are often seen carrying acorns to their winter stores.	RB
MAGPIE *Pica pica* Very common everywhere and hard to miss.	RB
CHOUGH *Pyrrhocorax pyrrhocorax* Resident in the west on the south Gower coast, breeding at traditional sites. In the east, a resident pair has been present for several years in the coastal strip from Nash (53) to Ogmore (52), breeding successfully for the first time in 2006. Can be seen in winter on the Heritage Coast.	RB
JACKDAW *Corvus monedula* Common everywhere.	RB
ROOK *Corvus frugilegus* There are many rookeries in the county, making them quite easy to find in summer. In winter they tend to form roving flocks in farmland areas of the Vale of Glamorgan in particular e.g. Colwinston.	RB
CARRION CROW *Corvus corone* Common, may be encountered anywhere.	RB
RAVEN *Corvus corax* Has bred in Central Cardiff on the City Hall clock tower. Elsewhere increasing. Breeds early in the year, usually in quarries and on rocky coasts. Large congregations occur in the Merthyr, Bargoed and Aberdare (34) areas e.g. Blaencanaid roost has over 200 (24).	RB

STARLING *Sturnus vulgaris* Common, especially in autumn and winter, with huge roost flocks at certain locations e.g. KNNR (1) reed beds - performing spectacular aerial shows at dusk	RB
ROSE–COLOURED STARLING *Sturnus roseus* Rare. Just 12 records. They usually associate with starling flocks in autumn. The first was in Swansea in 1836. Most are juvs. The 2003 summer-plumaged male at Port Talbot in late Jun. and early Jul. was atypical.	AV
HOUSE SPARROW *Passer domesticus* Still the commonest garden bird in the county. Not suffering the rapid decline of other areas. Numbers appear stable in Wales. Increasingly being seen on farmland rather than towns.	RB
TREE SPARROW *Passer montanus* Very local and now rare. In the west they are scarce but there are consistent winter reports from the Pilton Green area. Elsewhere numbers swell in winter when they join with finch flocks. In summer in the east, Monkton (53) and Pendoylan Moor are the most regular haunts and there is a very small breeding colony in nest boxes at the Monkton farms. There are winter feeding programmes at Newton Fm., Gower (44) and Monknash.	RB
CHAFFINCH *Fringilla coelebs* Very common and hard to miss.	RB
BRAMBLING *Fringilla montifringilla* Winter visitor, usually in small numbers. They favour Beech woodlands, feasting on fallen mast. Often found amongst finch flocks (particularly with the similar Chaffinch). Occasionally large flocks can erupt out of continental Europe.. Fforest Ganol/Fforest Fawr (23) had c. 1000 in the winter of 2007/8, which was part of a large invasion into the UK.	WV
GREENFINCH *Carduelis chloris* Widespread garden bird, visiting feeders in winter. Less gregarious in the summer . Easy to locate due to distinctive 'squeeze' calls.	RB
GOLDFINCH *Carduelis carduelis* Fairly ubiquitous. They typically form small to medium sized flocks (charms) in the post-breeding period and winter. Becoming more regular at garden bird tables that offer nyjer seed.	RB
SISKIN *Carduelis spinus* Relatively numerous, especially in cold winters. Occurs in roving tit flocks at Forest Fm. and Glamorgan Canal (22) associating with Redpoll. Parc Cwm Darran (12) holds a large wintering flock. In summer, breeding birds are present in conifers throughout the northern half of the county e.g. Llynfi Valley (6). They often visit garden feeding stations, especially in wet weather, when pine cones are swollen and more difficult to prise open.	RB
LINNET *Carduelis cannabina* Locally quite common, especially at coastal sites in spring and autumn, reflecting its migrant status. Many also breed however.	RB

TWITE *Carduelis flavirostris* Very uncommon. The last seen were at high altitude, over-wintering at the Werfa masts from Oct. 2003. They normally favour coastal salt marsh habitats however.	11-2 WV
LESSER REDPOLL *Carduelis cabaret* They breed in small numbers at Llanwonno and sites further north such as Parc Cwm Dare (34) and Garwnant (27). They are most numerous in winter, when quite large flocks of up to c. 100 can be seen at some sites e.g. Forest Fm./Glamorgan Canal (22) Taff Valley forests and around Maesteg (5/6). They prefer Alder trees.	RB
COMMON CROSSBILL *Loxia curvirostra* Regularly seen at Mynydd Margam (29) and Llanwonno (33), where they may breed. They are probably present in all conifer plantations e.g. Garwnant (27) Maesteg and Whiteford Pt. (41) Very local and often numerous.	RB
BULLFINCH *Pyrrhula pyrrhula* A farmland species and more recently a garden visitor. Nowhere common but often seen in the lanes of the Gower, Vale of Glamorgan and Rhondda Cynon Taff, where they nest in hedgerows. In winter, can form small flocks of about a dozen individuals in 'family' parties.	RB
HAWFINCH *Coccothraustes coccothraustes* Uncommon. They prefer Hornbeam woodlands e.g. Fforest Ganol (23), Cefn Onn (10) area, the Caerphilly ridge (11). Have been seen in Bute Park (17) and Forest Fm.(22).	RB
LAPLAND BUNTING *Calcarius lapponicus* Very uncommon, with fewer than 40 records. Almost annual on Gower e.g. Cwm Ivy (41). Several have been reported at Sker Fm.(1) fields. They are usually picked up by their call as they fly over.	AV
SNOW BUNTING *Plectrophenax nivalis* Very uncommon but almost annual. Has recently occurred on autumn migration at Ogmore (52) and Nash Pt. (53).	PM,WV
YELLOWHAMMER *Emberiza citronella* Quite common on farmland in Gower at Rhossili (43), Cefn Bryn and Pilton (44). They breed in pastoral localities but are becoming scarce and very localised. In the east, the Vale is the most likely area to see them. Recently they have been attracted to the winter feeding stations at Ty 'n -y-Caeau and Lan Fms., Monknash (53).	RB
CIRL BUNTING *Emberiza cirlus* Historic records only.	
ORTOLAN BUNTING *Emberiza hortulana* Rare with fewer than 20 records. Most likely in autumn at coastal sites such as Lavernock Pt. (50).	8-9 AV
REED BUNTING *Emberiza schoeniclus* Locally common at lake and reed bed locations throughout. Sometimes visits garden feeders in winter. May be encountered at any altitude. Frequent at the Cosmeston Lakes feeding stations (49) in winter.	RB
CORN BUNTING *Emberiza calandra* Very rare. Probably lost as a breeding species from the whole of Wales.	AV

Table 2 : Rare birds recorded in Glamorgan
(i.e. those with 5 or fewer records)

Species	Occurrences
AMERICAN WIGEON *Anas americana*	4 (possibly 5) records. The first two were both at KNNR (1) Oct.-Nov. 1975 and Oct.-Nov. 1985. The third and fourth were in CBWR (14) in Apr. 2002 with another there from May-Jun. 2006.
GREEN-WINGED TEAL *Anas carolinensis*	2 records. First recorded at KNNR (1) in Nov. 1981 with another at Oxwich Marsh (40) Jan.-Feb. 1983.
REDHEAD *Aythya americana*	1 record. This individual graced KNNR (1) in winter 2001, 2002, 2003 & 2004. It was also seen briefly at Cosmeston (49) & Llanishen/Lisvane Res. (19) both Feb. 2003 and at Llanilid in Mar. 2004.
LESSER SCAUP *Aythya affinis*	1 record. First located at Cosmeston Lakes (49) in Dec. 2008, later re-located in CBWR (14).
PIED-BILLED GREBE *Podylimbus podiceps*	3 records. (possibly 2) The first record was at KNNR (1), Jan.-Apr. 1987. Possibly the same individual returned there in Oct. 1987 and remained until Apr. 1988. Another was at Cosmeston Lakes (49) in Feb. 1999.
GREAT SHEARWATER *Puffinus gravis*	3 records involving 4 individuals. 1 off Port Eynon (45) in Aug. 1973, 1 off Mumbles (39) in July 1981 and 2 off Nash Pt. (53) in Aug 1986.
FRIGATEBIRD *Fregata sp.*	A Frigatebird sp. was seen over Flat Holm in Nov. 2005. (N.B. A Magnificent Frigatebird was found moribund in Shropshire the following day).
NIGHT HERON *Nycticorax nycticorax*	4 records, though none since 1990. The first was at Oxwich in June 1956 whilst the second visited ENR (28) in Nov. 1989. Probably the same bird (a juv.) was seen at Roath Park (20) in Nov. 1989 and later re-located at Cyncoed in Jan 1990. The Wernhalog bird on Gower in March 1990 was considered to be the same individual. A further 2 were at Oxwich (40) in Apr.-May 1990.
SQUACCO HERON *Ardeola ralloides*	3 records. The first was in Porthcawl (2) in May 1954. The second at KNNR (1) in June 1994 with the last in Cardiff at Lamby Lake (16) and later relocated at Cors Crychydd Reen (15) in June 2003.

CATTLE EGRET *Bubulcus ibis*	2 records. The first was at KNNR (1) in Nov. 2007, the second was at Hunts Farm, Gower in Feb/Mar 2008.
GREAT WHITE EGRET *Ardea alba*	4 (possibly 5) records. The first was at KNNR (1) in Aug. 1995. Another was at the Kenfig River mouth in Jul. 1997. One flew over Flat Holm in Sep. 2002. There was a long staying individual along the North Gower coast (42) from May 2004 to Aug. 2005.
GLOSSY IBIS *Plegadis falcinellus*	1 record at Skew Bridge in Oct. 1986.
BLACK KITE *Milvus migrans*	3 records. All are April/May records. The first was in 1979, between Overton and Paviland (44) with another over Cardiff in May of the same year.. The third was at KNNR (1) in Apr. 2003.
WHITE-TAILED EAGLE *Haliaeetus albicilla*	No recent records. The last was in 1859.
GOLDEN EAGLE *Aquila chrysaetos*	Only 1 historic record from Gower in 1864.
SORA *Porzana carolina*	1 record from Cardiff Docks in 1888.
LITTLE CRAKE *Porzans parva*	2 records. The first was in 1839. The second was at Llangennith Moors in Jan. 1967.
BAILLON'S CRAKE *Porzana pusilla*	1 record from Llantwit Major in Feb. 1976.
LITTLE BUSTARD *Tetrax tetrax*	1 record from Gileston (48) in Nov. 1885.
GREAT BUSTARD *Otis tarda*	1 record from Pontardawe in Dec. 1902.
BLACK-WINGED STILT *Himantopus himantopus*	1 record from KNNR (1) in Apr/May 2008.
COLLARED PRATINCOLE *Glareola pratincola*	1 record at Dalton's Pt. (42) in May 1973.
SOCIABLE PLOVER *Vanellus gregarius*	1 record from Jersey Marine in Oct. 1984.
SEMIPALMATED SANDPIPER *Calidris pusilla*	2 records, both from Ogmore Est. (52) in Sep. 1990 and 2001.
TEMMINCK'S STINT *Calidris temminckii*	3 records involving 4 individuals. The first was at Aberthaw (48) in Aug. 1974. 2 were at Blackpill (39) in May 1982. The last was at KNNR (1) in May 2005.
LEAST SANDPIPER *Calidris minutilla*	1 record from Aberthaw (48) in Sep. 1972.
WHITE-RUMPED SANDPIPER *Calidris fuscicollis*	3 records. First at Blackpill (39) in Sep. 1957, secondly at Swansea Docks in Mar. 1970. Lastly at KNNR (1) in Oct 2007.

BAIRD'S SANDPIPER *Calidris bairdii*	2 records. First at Aberthaw (48) in Sep. 1972. The second was at Whiteford (41) in Aug. 1975.
BUFF-BREASTED SANDPIPER *Tryngites subruficollis*	5 records, all in Sep. The first was at Burry Holms in 1977, then recorded from Rumney Great Wharf (15) in 1978 and 1980 and Sker Pt. (1) in 1983 and 1992.
LONG-BILLED DOWITCHER *Limnodromus scolopaceus*	1 record from the Rhymney Est. (15) in Apr. 1989.
LITTLE WHIMBREL *Numenius minutus*	1 record – the first for Great Britain and only the second Western Palearctic record was at Sker Fm. (1) from 30th Aug. to 6th Sep. 1982.
SPOTTED SANDPIPER *Actitis macularius*	3 records. The first was at Nicholaston Pill (40) in Aug 1973. The next was at Aberthaw in Aug. 1974 and the third over-wintered at Lisvane Res. (19) from Oct. 2007 to Apr. 2008.
LESSER YELLOWLEGS *Tringa flavipes*	1 record from Oxwich (40) in 1953.
IVORY GULL *Pagophila eburnea*	2 records. The first was at Gileston (48) on 2nd Jan 1998 and the second occurred at Blackpill (39) from late Nov. to early Dec. 2002.
ROSS'S GULL *Rhodostethia rosea*	1 record from Blackpill (39), Feb. 2002.
LAUGHING GULL *Larus atricilla*	3 records, all concerning 1st winter birds. The first was at Newton Pt. (2) in Sep. 1988. A second was found at Pink Bay (2) in Nov. 2005, staying in the Porthcawl area until Jan. 2006. The last was at Berges Is. (41) on 10th Nov. 2006, subsequently at Port Eynon (45) on 11th and finally at Swansea Docks on 15th.
FRANKLIN'S GULL *Larus pipixcan*	2 records - both adults. The first was at ENR (28). from 28th Oct. to 1st Nov. 1998. Secondly at Blackpill (39) in July 1999.
BRIDLED TERN *Onychoprion anaethetus*	1 record. Found dead at Three Cliff Bay on Gower in Sep.1954.
GULL-BILLED TERN *Gelochelidon nilotica*	2 records. One at ENR (28) and another at Whiteford Sands (40) in Sep. 1996.
CASPIAN TERN *Hydroprogne caspia*	3 records. The first was at Blackpill (39) in Aug. 1973, then at KNNR (1) in Apr. 1989 and the third at ENR (28) in Aug. 1997.
WHISKERED TERN *Childonias hybrida*	3 records involving 4 individuals. 2 were at Blackpill (39) in May 1974. Another was at ENR (28). in Sep. 1974. Lastly at KNNR (1) in May 2008.

ROYAL TERN *Sterna maxima*	2 records – both were 1st winter birds. KNNR (1) in Nov. 1979 and Mumbles (39) in Dec. 1987.
PALLAS'S SANDGROUSE *Syrrhaptes paradoxus*	Two historical records both in 1888: 2 at Fonmon and 16 on Llanrhidian Marsh (42).
SNOWY OWL *Bubo scandiacus*	1 record from Penarth Moors in Mar. 1972.
EAGLE OWL *Bubo bubo*	See appendix.
EUROPEAN ROLLER *Coracias garrulus*	1 record from Wernffrwd, Gower (42) in Aug. 2007.
SHORT-TOED LARK *Calandrella brachydactyla*	1 record from KNNR (1) in May 2008.
RED-RUMPED SWALLOW *Cecropis daurica*	1 record. One at ENR (28) in Aug. 1973.
TAWNY PIPIT *Anthus campestris*	2 records. The first was from Lavernock Pt. (50) in Oct.-Nov. 1967 whilst the second was at Nash Pt. (53) in Aug. 1991.
RED-THROATED PIPIT *Anthus cervinus*	1 record from KNNR (1) in May 1992.
BLUETHROAT *Luscinia svecica*	2 records. The first from KNNR (1) in Sep. 1970, then at Whiteford Pt. (41) in Oct. 2001.
DESERT WHEATEAR *Oenanthe deserti*	1 record from Penclawdd (42) in Nov. 1992.
BLACK-THROATED THRUSH *Turdus ruficollis atrogularis*	1 record from Townhill, Swansea in Jan. 2006.
SAVI'S WARBLER *Locustella luscinioides*	1 record from Oxwich (40) in May 1987.
ICTERINE WARBLER *Hippolais icterina*	5 records. Firstly from Lavernock Pt. (50) in Sep. 1978, Cosmeston Lakes (49) in Nov. 1982, Port Eynon (45) in Sep. 1987 and ringed on Flat Holm Aug. 1995. Also at Mewslade (44) on Gower in Sep. 2006.
MELODIOUS WARBLER *Hippolais polyglotta*	4 records. Firstly from Nash Pt. (53) in Sep. 1993, Llanmadoc in Oct. 1995, Glamorgan Coast in Oct. 1998 and Porthcawl (2) in May 2006.
BARRED WARBLER *Sylvia nisoria*	4 records. Three of the four have been at KNNR (1) and all in Sep. in 1979, 1994 and 2004. The only non-KNNR (1) record was at Nash Pt. in 1993.
PALLAS'S WARBLER *Phylloscopus proregulus*	4 records. Whitchurch, Cardiff in Nov. 1994, Aberaman in Dec. 1994, KNNR (1) in Dec. 2000 and Middleton (44), the last being on Gower in Oct. 2006.
BONELLI'S WARBLER *Phylloscopus sp.*	See appendix.

PENDULINE TIT *Remiz pendulinus*	1 occurrence. At least 2 (possibly 3 birds) were at KNNR (1) from Nov. 1996 to Mar. 1997.
NUTCRACKER *Nucrifraga caryocatactes*	2 records. One was killed near Swansea before 1870. The only other record was from Cwm Ivy (41) on Gower in Aug. 1968.
SERIN *Serinus serinus*	1 record of a male at KNNR (1) in Mar. 1982.
MEALY REDPOLL *Carduelis flammea*	3 records. Cardiff c.1860-90, Llantwit Fardre in Mar. 1986 and Llanedeyrn, Cardiff in Jan. 1987.
COMMON ROSEFINCH *Carpodacus erythrinus*	2 records. The first was at Rhossili (43) in Nov. 2004, the second was at Mewslade in Oct. 2007.
LITTLE BUNTING *Emberiza pusilla*	2 records. The first was from Oxwich Marsh (40) in Sep. 1957. The second was trapped and ringed at Mewslade on Gower in Nov. 2005.

Appendix :

- A skua that was found on Gower on 3rd Feb. 2002 and later taken into care was initially considered to be a Falklands Brown Skua, which, if verified, would have represented the second record for Britain. However recent research has indicated that it might have been a South Polar Skua. To date the record has not been verified by BOURC or BBRC.
- Eagle Owls have been reported from Maesteg, Bridgend, Cefn Cribwr, Merthyr Vale and Treoes. All are considered to be escaped birds.
- Bonelli's Warbler. 1 record from Lavernock Pt. in Aug.1963. With the BOURC split into western/eastern races – this record is now downgraded to *sp.* only. So it should be presumed to be 'Western Bonelli's Warbler' only.

*Footnote : List completed in July 2009.

Useful birding information

1. Bird watchers' code of conduct
2. Contacts
3. Bibliography and references
4. Glamorgan checklist

Black-tailed Godwits – Bob Mitchell

1. Bird watchers' code of conduct

1. Whatever your interest, be it photography, sketching, ringing, sound recording or just plain bird watching, the welfare of the birds must come first.

2. It is vital to protect habitats. Ensure your activities don't cause damage.

3. Keep disturbance to a minimum. Tolerance levels vary from species to species. It is safer to keep your distance. Birds should not be disturbed at the nest. It may give predators the opportunity to steal eggs or chicks. In cold weather, any disturbance may cause birds to use up vital energy supplies.

4. If you discover a rare bird, inform the County Recorder. Think about the interests of wildlife and local people before passing on news. This is especially important if you suspect breeding. Initially, it is probably best to keep the information secret in order to minimise disturbance or the risk of egg collectors discovering the nest.

5. Know the law and the rules for visiting the countryside. The bird protection laws are a result of hard campaigning. As birdwatchers, we must abide by them at all times. If you suspect illegal activities are taking place, inform your local Wildlife Crime Officer.

6. Respect the rights of landowners. Don't enter land without permission and comply with any permit schemes. If leading a group, it is advisable to give advance notice of your visit.

7. Have consideration for other bird watchers. Try not to disrupt their activities or scare away the birds they are watching. Many other people 'use' the countryside. Try not to interfere with their activities.

8. Record keeping is important. Much of our knowledge about birds comes from the record keeping of our predecessors. Make a point of sending records to the County Recorder.

9. If bird watching abroad, be sure to adhere to local laws.

10. Become a bird watching ambassador. Promote your hobby.

2. Contacts

The growth of the internet has made the acquisition of information much easier nowadays. Many organisations now have their own web pages. We hope the following local contact addresses are of use. Such lists obviously change over time. Details are thought to be correct at the time of going to press.

Editors : Alan Rosney 01443 841555 alan_rosney@glamorganbirds.org.uk
Richard Smith 01443 205816 rgsmith@birdpix.freeserve.co.uk

East Glamorgan Recorder : Geri Thomas 01443 836949/07984591983
geri_thomas@glamorganbirds.org.uk

West Glamorgan Recorder : Rob Taylor 01792 464780
rob_taylor@glamorganbirds.org.uk

Glamorgan Bird Club : John Wilson 02920 339424/07742728069
john_wilson@glamorganbirds.org.uk

Gower Ornithological Society : Heather Coats 01639 751020
See glamorganbirds website

BTO Representative East Glamorgan : Wayne Morris 01443 430284
waynemorris@tiscali.co.uk

BTO Representative West Glamorgan : Bob Howells 01792 405363
bobhowells31@hotmail.com

RSPB Cardiff local group : Joy Lyman 02920 770031
joy@lyman.plus.com

RSPB Swansea local group : Maggie Cornelius 01792 229244
maggie@westglam-rspb.org.uk

Wildlife Trust for South and West Wales : 01656 724100
welshwildilfe.org.

Gower Bird Hospital : 01792 371630
info@gowerbirdhospital.org.uk

Glamorgan Wildlife Photography Group : Paul Bowden 02920 813044
bowden@cf.ac.uk
Graham Duff 02920 398019 mem79@talktalk.net

3. Bibliography and references

Where to Watch Birds in Eastern Glamorgan- GBC (1998)
Eastern Glamorgan Bird Reports   - GBC (Annual)
Gower Birds   - GOS (Annual)
The Birds of Glamorgan   - Hurford & Lansdown (NMW 1995)
The Birds of Cardiff   - David Gilmore (GBC 2006)
The Birds of Bridgend   - Bridgend CBC (GBC 2001)
The Birds of the Caerphilly Basin   - Neville Davies (GBC 2008)
Discover Birds Around Caerphilly   - Caerphilly CBC/CCW
A Guide to Gower Birds   - Grenfell & Thomas (1982)
How to be a Bad Birdwatcher   - Simon Barnes (Short Books 2004)
Bearded Tit   - Rory McGrath (Ebury Press 2008)
Where to go for Wildlife in Glamorgan   - Nigel Ajax Lewis (GWT 1991)

Glamorgan checklist

MUTE SWAN					
BEWICK'S SWAN					
WHOOPER SWAN					
BEAN GOOSE					
PINK - FOOTED GOOSE					
WHITE - FRONTED GOOSE					
GREYLAG GOOSE					
CANADA GOOSE					
BARNACLE GOOSE					
BRENT GOOSE					
SHELDUCK					
MANDARIN DUCK					
WIGEON					
AMERICAN WIGEON					
GADWALL					
TEAL					
GREEN - WINGED TEAL					
MALLARD					
PINTAIL					
GARGANEY					
SHOVELER					
REDHEAD					
RED - CRESTED POCHARD					
POCHARD					
RING - NECKED DUCK					
FERRUGINOUS DUCK					
TUFTED DUCK					
SCAUP					
LESSER SCAUP					
EIDER					
LONG - TAILED DUCK					
SCOTER					
SURF SCOTER					
VELVET SCOTER					
GOLDENEYE					
SMEW					
RED - BREASTED MERGANSER					
GOOSANDER					
RUDDY DUCK					
RED GROUSE					
RED - LEGGED PARTRIDGE					
GREY PARTRIDGE					
QUAIL					
PHEASANT					

RED –THROATED DIVER					
BLACK-THROATED DIVER					
GREAT NORTHERN DIVER					
PIED – BILLED GREBE					
LITTLE GREBE					
PIED - BILLED GREBE					
GREAT CRESTED GREBE					
RED - NECKED GREBE					
SLAVONIAN GREBE					
BLACK - NECKED GREBE					
FULMAR					
CORY'S SHEARWATER					
GREAT SHEARWATER					
SOOTY SHEARWATER					
MANX SHEARWATER					
BALEARIC SHEARWATER					
STORM – PETREL					
LEACH'S STORM – PETREL					
GANNET					
CORMORANT					
SHAG					
BITTERN					
LITTLE BITTERN					
BLACK – CROWNED NIGHT HERON					
SQUACCO HERON					
CATTLE EGRET					
LITTLE EGRET					
GREAT (WHITE) EGRET					
GREY HERON					
PURPLE HERON					
WHITE STORK					
GLOSSY IBIS					
SPOONBILL					
HONEY – BUZZARD					
BLACK KITE					
RED KITE					
WHITE – TAILED EAGLE					
MARSH HARRIER					
HEN HARRIER					
GOSHAWK					
SPARROWHAWK					
COMMON BUZZARD					
ROUGH – LEGGED BUZZARD					
GOLDEN EAGLE					
OSPREY					
KESTREL					
RED – FOOTED FALCON					

MERLIN					
HOBBY					
PEREGRINE FALCON					
WATER RAIL					
SPOTTED CRAKE					
SORA					
LITTLE CRAKE					
BAILLON'S CRAKE					
CORNCRAKE					
MOORHEN					
COOT					
CRANE					
LITTLE BUSTARD					
GREAT BUSTARD					
OYSTERCATCHER					
BLACK – WINGED STILT					
AVOCET					
STONE - CURLEW					
COLLARED PRATINCOLE					
LITTLE RINGED PLOVER					
RINGED PLOVER					
KENTISH PLOVER					
DOTTEREL					
GOLDEN PLOVER					
GREY PLOVER					
SOCIABLE PLOVER					
LAPWING					
KNOT					
SANDERLING					
SEMIPALMATED SANDPIPER					
LITTLE STINT					
TEMMINCK'S STINT					
LEAST SANDPIPER					
WHITE – RUMPED SANDPIPER					
BAIRD'S SANDPIPER					
PECTORAL SANDPIPER					
CURLEW SANDPIPER					
PURPLE SANDPIPER					
DUNLIN					
BUFF – BREASTED SANDPIPER					
RUFF					
JACK SNIPE					
SNIPE					
LONG – BILLED DOWITCHER					
WOODCOCK					
BLACK - TAILED GODWIT					
BAR - TAILED GODWIT					

LITTLE WHIMBREL					
WHIMBREL					
CURLEW					
SPOTTED REDSHANK					
REDSHANK					
GREENSHANK					
LESSER YELLOWLEGS					
GREEN SANDPIPER					
WOOD SANDPIPER					
COMMON SANDPIPER					
SPOTTED SANDPIPER					
TURNSTONE					
RED - NECKED PHALAROPE					
GREY PHALAROPE					
POMARINE SKUA					
ARCTIC SKUA					
LONG - TAILED SKUA					
BROWN SKUA					
GREAT SKUA					
MEDITERRANEAN GULL					
LAUGHING GULL					
LITTLE GULL					
SABINE'S GULL					
BONAPATRE'S GULL					
BLACK - HEADED GULL					
RING - BILLED GULL					
COMMON GULL					
LESSER BLACK - BACKED GULL					
HERRING GULL					
YELLOW - LEGGED GULL					
ICELAND GULL					
GLAUCOUS GULL					
GREAT BLACK - BACKED GULL					
ROSS'S GULL					
KITTIWAKE					
IVORY GULL					
FRANKLIN'S GULL					
GULL – BILLED TERN					
CASPIAN TERN					
ROYAL TERN					
SANDWICH TERN					
ROSEATE TERN					
COMMON TERN					
ARCTIC TERN					
BRIDLED TERN					
LITTLE TERN					
WHISKERED TERN					

BLACK TERN					
WHITE-WINGED TERN					
GUILLEMOT					
RAZORBILL					
LITTLE AUK					
PUFFIN					
PALLAS' SANDGROUSE					
ROCK DOVE					
STOCK DOVE					
WOOD PIGEON					
COLLARED DOVE					
TURTLE DOVE					
CUCKOO					
BARN OWL					
SNOWY OWL					
LITTLE OWL					
TAWNY OWL					
LONG - EARED OWL					
SHORT - EARED OWL					
NIGHTJAR					
SWIFT					
ALPINE SWIFT					
KINGFISHER					
BEE - EATER					
ROLLER					
HOOPOE					
WRYNECK					
GREEN WOODPECKER					
GREAT SPOTTED WOODPECKER					
LESSER SPOTTED WOODPECKER					
GREATER SHORT – TOED LARK					
WOODLARK					
SKYLARK					
SHORE LARK					
SAND MARTIN					
RED – RUMPED SWALLOW					
BARN SWALLOW					
HOUSE MARTIN					
RICHARD'S PIPIT					
TAWNY PIPIT					
TREE PIPIT					
MEADOW PIPIT					
RED – THROATED PIPIT					
ROCK PIPIT					
WATER PIPIT					
YELLOW WAGTAIL					
GREY WAGTAIL					

PIED WAGTAIL					
WAXWING					
DIPPER					
WREN					
DUNNOCK					
ROBIN					
NIGHTINGALE					
BLUETHROAT					
BLACK REDSTART					
REDSTART					
WHINCHAT					
STONECHAT					
WHEATEAR					
DESERT WHEATEAR					
RING OUZEL					
BLACKBIRD					
BLACK – THROATED THRUSH					
FIELDFARE					
SONG THRUSH					
REDWING					
MISTLE THRUSH					
CETTI'S WARBLER					
GRASSHOPPER WARBLER					
SAVI'S WARBLER					
AQUATIC WARBLER					
SEDGE WARBLER					
REED WARBLER					
ICTERINE WARBLER					
MELODIOUS WARBLER					
DARTFORD WARBLER					
BARRED WARBLER					
LESSER WHITETHROAT					
WHITETHROAT					
GARDEN WARBLER					
BLACKCAP					
PALLAS'S WARBLER					
YELLOW - BROWED WARBLER					
WOOD WARBLER					
CHIFFCHAFF					
WILLOW WARBLER					
GOLDCREST					
FIRECREST					
SPOTTED FLYCATCHER					
RED – BREASTED FLYCATCHER					
PIED FLYCATCHER					
BEARDED TIT					
LONG - TAILED TIT					

MAR.SH TIT				
WILLOW TIT				
COAL TIT				
BLUE TIT				
GREAT TIT				
PENDULINE TIT				
NUTHATCH				
TREECREEPER				
GOLDEN ORIOLE				
RED - BACKED SHRIKE				
WOODCHAT SHRIKE				
GREAT GREY SHRIKE				
JAY				
MAGPIE				
NUTCRACKER				
CHOUGH				
JACKDAW				
ROOK				
CARRION CROW				
HOODED CROW				
RAVEN				
STARLING				
ROSE – COLOURED STARLING				
HOUSE SPARROW				
TREE SPARROW				
CHAFFINCH				
BRAMBLING				
SERIN				
GREENFINCH				
GOLDFINCH				
SISKIN				
LINNET				
TWITE				
LESSER REDPOLL				
MEALY REDPOLL				
COMMON CROSSBILL				
COMMON ROSEFINCH				
BULLFINCH				
HAWFINCH				
LAPLAND BUNTING				
SNOW BUNTING				
YELLOWHAMMER				
CIRL BUNTING				
ORTOLAN BUNTING				
LITTLE BUNTING				
REED BUNTING				
CORN BUNTING				

Acknowledgements

Most of the site guides included in this publication have been provided by local bird watchers. The editors are greatly indebted to the following for their contributions :

Martin Bevan
David Carrington
Alex Coxhead
Paul Denning
Neil Edwards
Alastair Flannagan
Adrian Hopkins
N. Paul Roberts
Alan Rosney
Margaret Samuel
Bob Tallack

David Beveridge
Maurice Chown
Neville Davies
Clive Ellis
Mark Everett (Welsh Water)
David Gilmore
Wayne Morris
Colin Richards
John Samuel
Richard Smith
John Wilson

Thanks to Paul Seligman for proof-reading the text.